FACTORY-ORIGINAL
LAND ROVER
SERIES I, 80-INCH MODELS

FACTORY-ORIGINAL
LAND ROVER
SERIES I, 80-INCH MODELS

BY JAMES TAYLOR
PHOTOGRAPHY BY SIMON CLAY

Herridge & Sons

Published in 2021 by
Herridge & Sons Ltd
Lower Forda, Shebbear
Beaworthy, Devon EX21 5SY

© Copyright James Taylor 2021

Design: Muse Fine Art & Design

All rights reserved. No part of this publication may be reproduced in any form or by any means without the prior written permission of the publisher and the copyright holder.

ISBN 978-1-906133-90-0
Printed in China

CONTENTS

ACKNOWLEDGEMENTS 6

THE 80-INCH MODELS, 1948-1953 8

THE PRE-PRODUCTION LAND ROVERS 20

CHASSIS, AXLES, SUSPENSION, STEERING,
BRAKES, WHEELS & TYRES 29

ENGINE, TRANSMISSION & EXHAUST 43

BODYWORK (LOWER) 56

BODYWORK (UPPER) & CANVAS 75

ELECTRICAL ITEMS 84

INTERIOR AND TOOLS 92

THE TICKFORD STATION WAGONS 103

THE WELDER 117

FIRE ENGINES 122

OPTIONAL EQUIPMENT 130

MILITARY MODIFICATIONS – 80-INCH 144

CKD MODELS 150

GRIP, MINERVA AND TEMPO 153

ACKNOWLEDGEMENTS

Somewhere around 25 years ago, publisher Charles Herridge invited me to write a book about original specifications of the Series I Land Rovers. That book, *Original Land Rover Series I*, went on to sell very well. It also helped to highlight areas where not much detailed information was known and, over the years that followed, several dedicated individuals put in a great deal of research to improve the collective knowledge.

So even though a reprint of that first book was still selling, it was becoming increasingly clear that something new was needed. The large amount of new information that had been uncovered meant that a simple update would not be enough; a completely new book was necessary. It also became clear that there was so much that could now be said that a single volume would not be able to do it justice. We therefore agreed to create two volumes: this first one deals with the 80-inch types, and the second volume will cover the 86, 88, 107 and 109 models that followed them.

The purpose of the present book is to record as far as practicable the multiple changes in specification that affected the 80-inch Land Rovers built between 1948 and 1953. These changes matter to many enthusiasts when they are rebuilding a vehicle and trying to put it back to the condition it was in when it left the assembly line at the Rover factory.

There is a very understandable degree of satisfaction to be had from such an enterprise, but it is not an easy task. Large numbers of 80-inch models were modified when they became cheap and disposable, either with more modern components to keep them running or more extensively to turn them into triallers and off-road specials. Many will stay that way, probably for ever, and in my view it is far better that they should be used and enjoyed than discarded and scrapped. However, as interest in the earliest Land Rovers has increased, and as prices have increased with it (in some cases to quite extraordinary levels), there are many more people who want to try their hand at restoration. I hope this book will help them to understand what they are aiming for.

It would be impossible to record the name of everybody who has contributed to the knowledge that has gone into this book. So instead I will single out a small number of people who helped specifically during the time I was writing it.

Mike Bishop has done a huge amount of research on the 80-inch models; Alex Massey and Rob Sprason at the CKD Shop have gone into exquisite detail to ensure that their products for restorers are as right as it is possible to make them; and my colleague Peter Galilee very kindly offered to comment on drafts of the manuscript (and then probably wished he hadn't). John Smith filled in some details that I could not find elsewhere.

The main photographic effort came from Simon Clay, with whom I have worked for many years. Some photographs are my own (and there are no prizes for identifying which those are), and the provenance of others is identified in the captions where appropriate.

Many different vehicles figure in the photographs, and to list the identity of every one of them would take up too much space here. However, my special thanks must go to the owners of the following:

1948 pre-production	R14 HNX 444	Mike Rivett
1948 model	R86-0027 (chassis)	Adam Bennett
1948 model	R86-1164	Alex Massey
1948 models	NNU 581	
	NNU 582	Robert Sargeant
1948 Tickford	KAD 749	Mike Street
1949 model	GAK 58	The CKD Shop
1950 Tickford	MST 494	Mike Rivett
1951 Welder	NXS 767	Mike Rivett
1953 AA vehicle	(chassis)	Nick Parr
1953 Fire Engine	3610-2353 FF 8721	Mike Rivett
Brockhouse trailer	BT8 4600	Mike Rivett

James Taylor
Oxfordshire, May 2021

THE 80-INCH MODELS, 1948-1953

The pre-production models were built in the first half of 1948. This is R14, owned by Mike Rivett, and it shows the light green paint used on the very first Land Rovers.

The story of the Land Rover's origins is worth retelling at the start of a book like this one in order to provide some context, although the main objective of the pages that follow is to give guidance on the way these vehicles were when they were new.

Like other British car manufacturers, the Rover Company had suspended car manufacture during the Second World War and had devoted its efforts to building machines needed for the war – in Rover's case, mainly aircraft components. Even though some plans had existed for new saloon models when car production had been suspended in 1940, it was clear that both customer expectations and manufacturing conditions would be very different in the post-war world.

There would be a major change in the company's location, too. Enemy bombing in November 1940 had seriously damaged Rover's original manufacturing centre in Coventry, and in 1944 the Board of Directors decided to sell it. Meanwhile, the company had been managing a "shadow" aero engine factory at Solihull in the West Midlands on behalf of the government, and the offer of first refusal for it at the end of the war was too tempting to ignore. So although the government was not initially prepared to sell it outright, Rover was able to negotiate

a favourable lease and began to establish a new manufacturing base there during 1945.

With no viable new models, the company did the best it could, and updated some of the saloon cars it had been building in pre-war days to put them back into production. Meanwhile, design work went ahead on new products, because it was clear that these pre-war designs would not continue to attract customers for much longer. But there was an additional imperative: shortly after the end of the war, the British government announced that the country's manufacturers must give priority to overseas orders. The focus on overseas trade was intended to bring money into a Britain which had nearly bankrupted itself during the war, and the outlook was made even more bleak when the Ministry of Supply made clear that it would ration steel (which was in short supply as the country emerged from war), favouring those users who performed best in overseas trade.

Rover's existing saloons were too old-fashioned to compete with more modern designs (especially those from the USA) in overseas markets, and it would be some time before their more modern replacements were ready. By late 1946 – a year after the war's end – the problem was a pressing one. That winter proved to be one of the hardest on record in Britain, and many of the trees blew down in the long drive leading up to Blackdown Manor, the Midlands home of Rover's Chief Engineer Maurice Wilks. They made access to the main road difficult, and so Wilks visited the local military surplus dump and bought himself a Loyd Carrier – a tracked vehicle that was not daunted by mud or snow and had the power to haul the fallen trees out of the way.

Not long after that, one of Wilks' neighbours showed him an Army surplus Jeep he had bought; Wilks was fascinated by it, and the two men swapped vehicles. Wilks used the Jeep to clear trees at Blackdown Manor, and he took it off to the cottage he had bought as a holiday home on Anglesey. By Easter 1947, he was sure that Rover could make a similar vehicle, focusing on agricultural and light industrial users (although he must have realised that it would have military uses too), and that it could be built with some of the major components already designed for the next generation of Rover cars.

He discussed his idea with some of his colleagues at Rover – most notably his brother, Spencer Wilks, who was the company's Managing Director – and during September obtained agreement from the Rover Board to develop the vehicle for production. Within a month, it had been christened the Land Rover. It was an entirely new venture for the Rover Company, and it appears

Even though the pre-production models very much anticipated the production design, there were multiple differences between the two – and among the pre-production models themselves – as the next Chapter explains

that to some extent it was considered as a temporary expedient until normal trading conditions returned and the company could focus fully on its traditional cars.

So it was that the Rover designers and engineers began in autumn 1947 to design and develop this new vehicle for production at the earliest possible opportunity. Although it took another nine months or so before production began in earnest, representative pre-production models were ready in time for an international announcement at the Amsterdam Show that opened on 30 April. As is well known, the Land Rover was an immediate success.

Changes and cautions

The new model had been prepared in record time. Rover had been able to make use of the new four-cylinder engine that they had already drawn up for their new saloon cars, and they arranged for the body and chassis to be easily constructed by hand so that they would not have to wait for special press tools to be made. They created the main chassis members by welding four flat pieces of steel together at their edges to create a simple but immensely strong box-section, and wherever possible they used body panels that were flat or had only a single curvature. The assembly operation was made as simple as possible, by using components suitable for both LHD and RHD vehicles (and redundant holes for fixings were simply blanked off), while rivets, bolts and screws enabled the new vehicle to be built by assembly line staff with no experience of welding.

The concept was driven through with determination, and the Land-Rover (the name initially had a hyphen) was ready and fit for purpose in summer 1948. Yet it is clear from the number of changes that Rover made on production over the next three years that there was plenty of development work still to be done. On the whole, these changes were less associated with the functioning of the vehicle than they were with manufacturing and assembly. Our understanding of the development process on production in the early days is clouded because many pre-production spares seem to have been used up on the first 150 or so Land Rovers. The result was that more considered production versions appeared only gradually during this period. There were few well-defined changeover points; revised components appeared as they were needed and as they became available.

At the same time, the assembly line staff were identifying more efficient ways of building the vehicle, and these were introduced on production as and when the new solutions were ready. Almost none of these changes were mentioned in service literature of the time, as they made no difference to either dealer mechanics or home mechanics who maintained the vehicles.

This constant stream of minor changes and the reasons behind them are a major part of the fascination of the early Land Rovers. Just by thinking about why an elongated hole in a pressing replaced a simple circular hole, it is possible

Land Rovers were green, green or green, except for a few built to special order. This late 1948 model was delivered to the Derby Fire Brigade for support duties, and Rover obligingly painted it red and delivered it with red seats. The genuine Land Rover fire engine was still in the future. The vehicle belongs to Robert Sargeant, who has restored it to original condition.

THE 80-INCH MODELS, 1948-1953

This 1949 model is many enthusiasts' vision of a classic 80-inch Land Rover. It has been meticulously restored to original condition by the CKD Shop.

By the time this vehicle was built, the standard body colour had changed to Deep Bronze Green and the chassis was painted to match.

FACTORY-ORIGINAL LAND ROVER SERIES I, 80-INCH MODELS

The restorer's dilemma: these two 1949 models were both delivered new to the Derby Fire Brigade. NNU 582 has been restored to original ex-factory condition, and NNU 581 has been left with the multiple modifications it received in service, which included an upgrade to a 2-litre engine. There are valid reasons for both approaches to preserving an 80-inch Land Rover.

almost to reconnect with the staff on the assembly line and to hear them explaining that the elongated hole allowed for easier adjustment if manufacturing tolerances were a little wide. Being able to imagine the explanation conducted with a Brummie (strictly, Solihull) accent helps.

It is nevertheless important to note that this method of working on the assembly lines means that it is frequently impossible to give an exact changeover point from one type of component to its successor. It is possible to say that a change occurred at around a certain chassis number, but no more. Restorers should never forget that after a change had been made and recorded, somebody might have found another batch of the older components in the stores, and these would have been used up on the lines to avoid wastage. As a result the word "theoretically" occurs quite frequently in this book in connection was estimated changeover points.

In later service literature, and in the Parts Catalogues, Rover provided what look like clear changeover points in the form of chassis numbers. These should also be treated with caution. A good many are probably completely accurate, but others may have been established retrospectively, after the vehicles in question had not only been built but had been shipped to their destination and could no longer be checked.

The first set of what might be called planned changes was introduced in December 1948, after 1500 chassis had been built. In the mean time, the Station Wagon had become a production option. A far more visible change was from light "No2" Green to Deep Bronze Green in June 1949, and there would be countless other changes, both small and not so small, over the next two years. In fact, the specification of the Land Rover did not really settle down until 1951, when the much-reduced flow of minor modifications made clear that the company believed they had got it right at last. And just at that point, Rover decided to fit an enlarged 2-litre engine in place of the original 1.6-litre type....

The last 80-inch Land Rovers were built in mid-1953, and by that stage their larger successors were ready to enter production. These 86-inch models – and the later examples of the family that became known retrospectively as "Series I" types when their Series II successors arrived in 1958 – will be covered in a companion volume to this one.

THE 80-INCH MODELS, 1948-1953

The Station Wagon body was built for Rover by Salmons-Tickford at Newport Pagnell, using traditional coachbuilding methods. As a passenger-carrying vehicle, it attracted Purchase Tax, and that made it much too expensive to attract many British buyers. This 1950 model, owned by Mike Rivett, is the second to last example built, and was new to Ghana.

From mid-1950, Land Rovers took on a new frontal appearance with larger headlights that emerged through the grille. This 1951 model was built as a Mobile Welder and was originally exported to Australia. It belongs to Mike Rivett and was still under restoration when photographed.

THE 80-INCH MODELS, 1948-1953

When the factory-built Land Rover Fire Engine finally appeared, it was a most attractive looking machine that was ideal as a first-response tender for rural or factory use. This 1953 example was new to the Merioneth Fire Brigade in north Wales, and was supplied with the optional metal truck cab.

The Fire Engine carried a first-aid water tank, a fire pump and various hoses. It was never very numerous, and its construction probably caused Land Rover some headaches because of the need to incorporate specialist equipment provided from outside the company. This one belongs to Mike Rivett.

15

CHASSIS NUMBERS AND PRODUCTION TOTALS FOR 80-INCH LAND ROVERS

The chassis number of an 80-inch Land Rover was stamped into the top of the left-hand front engine mounting bracket. The chassis number was the same as the vehicle identification number.

On 1948-50 models, this number was stamped into a plate on the engine side of the bulkhead, on the left-hand side of the vehicle (that is, on the right when standing looking into the engine bay). On 1951-53 models (that is, those with selectable four-wheel drive), it was stamped into the transmission instruction plate that was screwed to the bulkhead just above the flywheel housing.

Chassis numbers consisted of two elements. The first was a prefix that identified the vehicle type and model-year of its construction. The second was a serial number. In this book, the two are separated by a hyphen for clarity, but this hyphen does not appear on the actual vehicles or in their documentation.

Model-years typically ran over two calendar years, from September to July, and there was no production in August while the staff took their annual holiday. A 1950 model might therefore have been built in either late 1949 or the first seven months of 1950. Inevitably, the demarcations were not always precise, and an exception was made for the first year of production. The "1948" basic models were built from July 1948 to January 1949, and the 1949 basic models entered production during February 1949. Production of the 1949 Station Wagons and Welders also began in early 1949.

On 1948, 1949 and 1950 models, the type prefix was preceded by an R for RHD or an L for LHD, as appropriate. From March 1950, the R was omitted on home market models, but was usually present on export types. This change took effect at chassis numbers 0611-0348, 0620-0265 and 0630-0001.

On very early chassis there is a four-digit number stamped into the left-hand engine mounting foot, alongside the chassis number but in smaller characters. This appears to be a sequential number allocated to early chassis frames and is not associated with the formal chassis number, although in some cases the number is quite close to the last four digits of that number.

The tables below show the chassis number sequences and production totals for all 80-inch Land Rovers. That there was no special identifying prefix for 1950 CKD models, which were numbered in the main sequences. There were two sequences for 1950 because production exceeded the quantities envisaged at the start of the year, and the numbers in the first sequence simply ran out.

1.6-LITRE MODELS, 1948-1951

There were 44,310 production 1.6-litre models, plus 48 pre-production vehicles. In addition, 50 production prototypes of the 2-litre model were built during the currency of the 1.6-litre type.

Note that the serial number shown here is preceded by an R or an L on all 1948-1950 models, and on later export models too. The letters indicate RHD or LHD respectively.

The despatch records include an entry for 0610-10000. This has been amended to read 0611-0000, and is separate from the entry for 0611-0001. The vehicle is recorded as going to Regent Motors in Australia, but it is unclear whether it really existed or there was simply a clerical error.

1948 Basic	86-0001 to 86-3000	3000
1949 Basic	866-3001 to 866-7920	7920
Station Wagon	867-0001 to 867-0070	70
Welder	868-0001 to 868-0010	10
		8000
1950 Basic	0610-0001 to 0610-9999	9999
	0611-0001 to 0611-5440	5440
Station Wagon	0620-0001 to 0620-0480	480
Welder	0630-0001 to 0630-0030	30
2-litre prototypes	0710-0001 to 0710-0050	50
		15,999
1951 Basic	1610-0001 to 1610-3971 Home market	3971
	1613-0001 to 1613-7601 LHD	7601
	1616-0001 to 1616-3268 RHD export	3268
	1663-0001 to 1663-0078 LHD, CKD	78*
	1666-0001 to 1666-2320 RHD, CKD	2320
Station Wagon	1623-0001 to 1623-0080 LHD	80
	1626-0001 to 1620-0020 RHD export	20
Welder	1630-0001 to 1630-0004 Home market	4
	1633-0001 to 1633-0007 LHD	7
	1636-0001 to 1636-0009 RHD export	9
		17,358

2-LITRE MODELS, 1952-1953

There were 40,869 production 2-litre models, plus a further 50 production prototypes built in 1950 (see above).

The 1952 2663-series and 1953 3663-series both included quantities of chassis that were shipped to Minerva in Belgium to receive special bodywork. The 1953 3613-series included batches that were shipped to West Germany for completion as Tempo models. For more information about the Minerva and Tempo vehicles, see the chapter covering these cars on page 153.

No records have been found for 1953 RHD CKD models, but the highest chassis number so far traced (in Australia) is 3666-2122, and this has been used in the table below.

1952 Basic	2610-0001 to 2610-5569 Home market	5569
	2613-0001 to 2613-6424 LHD	6424
	2616-0001 to 2613-3614 RHD export	3614
	2663-0001 to 2663-1985 LHD, CKD	1985
	2666-0001 to 2666-1092 RHD, CKD	1092
Welder	2630-0001 to 2630-0014 Home market	14
	2633-0001 to 2633-0013 LHD	13
	2636-0001 to 2636-0004 RHD export	4
		18,715
1953 Basic	3610-0001 to 3610-4122 Home market	4122
	3613-0001 to 3613-4613 LHD	4613
	3616-0001 to 3616-4007 RHD export	4007
	3663-0001 to 3663-7268 LHD, CKD	7268
	3666-0001 to 3666-2122 RHD, CKD	2122
Welder	3630-0001 to 3630-0008 Home market	8
	3633-0001 to 3633-0007 LHD	7
	3636-0001 to 3636-0007 RHD export	7
		22,154

* This figure has been traditionally quoted as 81, but the Despatch Department records held at Gaydon record only 78 chassis.

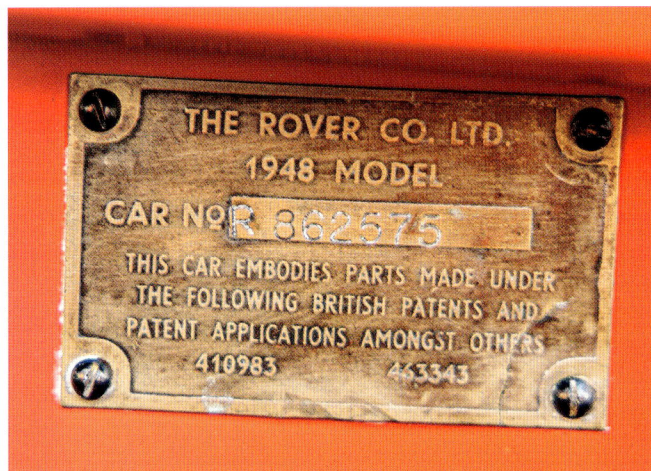

The early chassis plate was made of brass and was mounted on the engine side of the bulkhead. This one would originally have had a black background to the letters.

This is the later style of chassis plate, on a 1953 fire engine. It was attached to the bulkhead on the cab side.

Aluminium plates were introduced from late 1948, but there appears not to have been a clear changeover point, and the brass and aluminium types were in use together for some months.

The chassis number is stamped into the left-hand engine mounting foot. This one is R861164. On this late 1948 chassis, note the number in smaller characters to the left of it – 1256 in this case – which is thought to be a build number for the chassis frame itself.

SPECIFICATIONS FOR 80-INCH LAND ROVERS

Engines
1948-1950 models:
1595cc (69.5mm x 105mm) four-cylinder with overhead inlet and side exhaust valves; single Solex 32 PBI-2 carburettor.
6.8:1 compression ratio. 50bhp at 4000rpm and 80 lb ft at 2000rpm.
1951-1953 models:
1997cc (77.8mm x 105mm) four-cylinder with overhead inlet and side exhaust valves; single Solex 32 PBI-2 carburettor.
6.8:1 compression ratio. 52bhp at 4000rpm and 101 lb ft at 1500rpm.

Transmission:
1948-1950 models:
Permanent four-wheel drive with freewheel.
Four-speed main gearbox with synchromesh on 3rd and 4th gears only; ratios 3.00:1, 2.04:1, 1.47:1, 1.00:1, reverse 2.54:1.
Two-speed transfer gearbox; ratios 1.148:1 (High) and 2.89:1 (Low)
Axle ratio: 4.7:1 (first few hundred models with 4.88:1)
1951-1953 models:
Selectable four-wheel drive.
Four-speed main gearbox with synchromesh on 3rd and 4th gears only; ratios 3.00:1, 2.04:1, 1.38:1, 1.00:1, reverse 2.54:1.
Two-speed transfer gearbox; ratios 1.148:1 (High) and 2.89:1 (Low)
Axle ratio: 4.7:1

Suspension, steering and brakes:
Semi-elliptic leaf springs all round.
Recirculating-ball steering with 15:1 ratio.
Drum brakes (10in x 1.5in) on all four wheels;
separate drum-type transmission parking brake.

Electrical system:
12-volt, positive earth, with dynamo.

Dimensions:
Overall length:	132in (3353mm)
Wheelbase:	80in (2032mm)
Overall width:	61in (1549mm)
Unladen height:	70.5in (1971mm) with hood up
Track:	50in (1270mm)
Unladen weight:	2594 lb (1177kg)

Performance (with 1.6-litre engine):
0-40mph:	18secs
Maximum:	50mph approx (80.4km/h)
Fuel consumption:	24 mpg approx

Performance (with 2-litre engine):
0-50mph:	20.5secs
Maximum:	52mph approx (84km/h)
Fuel consumption:	24 mpg approx

COMPONENT DATING

Many components on an 80-inch Land Rover carry a date of manufacture, which may be stamped into the body of the item or into a tag attached to it. This date is typically in the format "7/49" (ie month and year), and may be found on radiators (a circular brass plate on the header tank) and wheel discs, among other items. Many Lucas electrical components carry a four-digit code, which gives the number of the week and the year (eg 25/50).

Glass, but not Perspex, fitted to these models can also be dated, assuming it is glass made by the original manufacturer, Triplex. This is not reliable as a method of dating the vehicle itself, because glass can be swapped between one Land Rover and another. However, it can be useful to determine whether the glass in question is likely to be original to the vehicle.

Triplex etched a code into their glass, and it can be found within the maker's mark that is usually easily visible. The code depends on a system of dots.

The year of manufacture is indicated by a dot (or no dot) below one of the letters of the word TOUGHENED, as below.

E	1948	T	1951
D	1949	O	1952
No dot	1950	U	1953

A further dot above the word TRIPLEX indicates the quarter of the year in which the glass was manufactured, as follows:

T	First quarter (January, February, March)
R	Second quarter (April, May, June)
E	Third quarter (July, August, September)
X	Fourth quarter (October, November, December).

This metal disc on the header tank gives the date of the radiator's manufacture; in this case, it is 11/48 (November 1948).

PRICES IN BRITAIN

April 1948   £450

November 1948   £540

This price increase reflected the inclusion as standard of several items initially listed as extra-cost options. These were the doors and sidescreens, the full-length canvas tilt, the two passenger seats, the bulkhead hand rail, a spare wheel with 600x 16 tyre, a starting handle, a towing plate for the drawbar, a pintle hook, and a socket and cable for trailer lighting.

December 1948   £750 plus £209 1s 8d Purchase Tax; total £959 1s 8d (Tickford Station Wagon)

November 1949   £564 10s 10d with Centre PTO and engine governor

December 1949   £995 with Bullows air compressor

January 1950   £825 for Mobile Welding Plant, exclusive of gas welding equipment

January 1952   £598

May 1953   £905 for Fire Engine (Detachable metal cab £25 11s 0d extra)

MATCHING NUMBERS?

With some makes of vehicle, the engine serial number and chassis serial number were always the same when the vehicles left the factory. This has led to a widespread belief that "matching numbers" are an indication that a vehicle still has its original engine.

The engine and chassis serial numbers of an 80-inch Land Rover very rarely matched, and if they did so, it was more by coincidence than anything else. Engines were assembled and numbered separately from chassis, and any number of factors ensured that the numbers were usually out of sequence when the two components were eventually united on the assembly lines.

As random examples from Rover Company records:

Chassis	Engine number
86-0039	86-0071
0610-2302	0610-2820
R0611-0326	0611-0561

WHERE DID THEY ALL GO?

The vast majority of 80-inch Land Rovers were shipped abroad, and only about 30% remained in Britain. No definitive list of export destinations exists, but the following list was current in January 1951 and shows Land Rover dealers in 103 different countries. Note that several countries have changed their names in more recent years. In a few cases, Land Rovers were not shipped in fully built form but rather in CKD form for assembly in the destination country.

Aden	El Salvador	Norway
Algeria	Eritrea	Panama
Argentina	Ethiopia	Paraguay
Australia	Fiji Islands	Persia
Austria	Finland	Persian Gulf (via Bahrain)
Barbados	France	Peru
Belgian Congo	French Equatorial Africa	Porto Rico
Belgium	French West Africa	Portugal
Bermuda	Gibraltar	Portuguese East Africa
Bolivia	Greece	Portuguese West Africa
Brazil	Guatemala	St Kitts
British East Africa	Holland	St Vincent
British Guiana	Honduras	Saudi Arabia
British Honduras	Iceland	Siam
British New Guinea	India	South Africa
British Somaliland	Indonesia	Southern Rhodesia
British West Africa	Iraq	South West Africa
Burma	Israel	Spain
Canada	Italy	Spanish Morocco
Canary Isles	Jamaica	Sudan (Anglo-Egyptian)
Caribbean (via Jamaica)	Japan	Sweden
Ceylon	Jordan	Switzerland
Chile	Kuwait	Syria
China	Lebanon	Trinidad
Colombia	Liberia	Tunisia
Costa Rica	Libya	Turkey
Cyprus	Madeira	Uruguay
Cuba	Malaya (Singapore)	USA
Cyrenaica	Malta & Gozo	Venezuela
Denmark	Mauritius	West Pakistan
Dominican Republic	Newfoundland	Yemen
Dutch Guiana	New Hebrides	Yugoslavia
Ecuador	New Zealand	
Egypt	Nicaragua	
Eire	Northern Rhodesia	

Known additions in later years were Mexico (CKD from 1952 season) and West Germany (semi-KD from 1953 season).

THE PRE-PRODUCTION LAND ROVERS

The 48 pre-production models that Rover built in the first half of 1948 have become a kind of Holy Grail for anyone interested in the early Land Rover. Fewer than half are known to survive – although the Land Rover community lives in hope, and this author was present at the remarkable rediscovery in 2015 of pre-production model number 7, which had been sitting unnoticed in a garden in Birmingham for many years. The known survivors are cherished by their owners, and each one has its own individual tale to tell.

Not that it is very easy to discover the full story behind any of these vehicles. It is even less easy to establish a detailed build specification because the Rover engineers' ideas were evolving as the vehicles were being built. Improvements were being suggested all the time, and as these were development vehicles, they were modified willy-nilly to meet the engineers' requirements. Probably no two were exactly the same when they were built, and many finished their time at Rover with a specification that was quite different from the one with which they started life. At least seven, for example, were converted from left-hand-drive to right-hand drive.

Some of the pre-production Land Rovers were used as demonstrators before production volumes had built up, and inevitably Rover modified these so that they were representative of the latest production standard. Two (numbers L29 and R30) were evaluated by the Ministry of Supply, which was then the purchasing agency for Britain's armed forces (and this would lead to large military orders later on). Two more (numbers L31 and R32) went to the National Institute for Agricultural Engineering, which wanted to test how well they really performed as agricultural vehicles. Three more went to Rover's overseas representatives to spread the knowledge of the new product, and four were temporarily exported to Europe for much the same reason. A few were sold to Rover employees when they were no longer needed for development work, and no doubt any damaged parts were replaced by current production items either at that stage or later on during ownership.

So this chapter can do no more than highlight some of the quirks of the pre-production Land Rovers, and to illustrate through that how the design evolved in remarkably quick time to enter production in summer 1948. What the subsequent chapters illustrate, and in very much more detail, is how that design continued to evolve over five years of production. In fact, it was constantly evolving in the first three years, and it was not really until mid-1951 and the arrival of the 2-litre models for the 1952 season that the specification can be said to have settled down. There were certainly far fewer design changes after that watershed.

The original plan had been to build 50 pre-production Land Rovers, which was a much higher number of prototypes than Rover normally built and was a reflection of their need to test a lot of new features in a very short time; this was, after all, a very different type of vehicle from the comfortable saloon cars that were traditional Rover fare. Even in the early 1960s, the company put the radically new P6 saloon into production after

This was R01 when relatively new. The picture shows that only the staples were present in the body sides, and also that the vehicle's identification number (it had not yet been registered) was painted on the rear cross-member.

THE PRE-PRODUCTION LAND ROVERS

building and testing only 15 prototypes! In practice, only 48 pre-production Land Rovers were built, and supposedly for the very good reason that the engineers did not need any more. By the time the last few were completed (by hand, on a temporary production line in a corner of the Assembly Shop at Solihull, in the building now known as the South Works), production models had begun to roll off the assembly lines, and any further development work could be more usefully and easily done on some of them.

The pre-production Land Rovers were all numbered in a simple prototype sequence between 01 and 48 (the number always consisted of two digits). These numbers were preceded by a letter R to indicate right-hand drive or an L to indicate left-hand drive. In cases where the steering position was changed from one to the other, the chassis retained its original serial number but was re-stamped with the appropriate prefix letter. Volume production of the Land Rover had not begun by the time Rover wanted to introduce its new model to the world, and so it was a pair of pre-production vehicles that did the job at the Amsterdam Motor Show in April 1948. On the Rover stand was L05, and outside the exhibition hall in the demonstration vehicles park was L03.

This is the legendary "Huey", more formally R01, the first pre-production Land Rover. It was originally restored using production parts, but is gradually being put back to its original condition. Note here, for example, that it has both staples and cleats for the hood fixing; early photographs confirm that it only had the staples when new.

FACTORY-ORIGINAL LAND ROVER SERIES 1, 80-INCH MODELS

R03 was a left-hand-drive pre-production model but has since been converted to right-hand drive. It was one of the two vehicles that introduced the Land Rover in Amsterdam at the end of April 1948. The large Land Rover emblem on the wing is believed to date from that time.

Identification (1): the chassis number is stamped, somewhat crudely, into a standard Rover car identification plate on the engine side of the bulkhead.

Identification (2): the number is also stamped into the engine mounting foot on the chassis. R07 started life as L07, and hammer marks around the prefix letter bear witness to the change.

22

The chassis number was also painted on the front cross-member, as here. Although most of the known examples seem to have been black, some were white and there was no standard style. R32 has the early type of bumper, welded to the chassis.

KEY FEATURES OF THE PRE-PRODUCTION MODELS

Chassis

The production chassis design was largely in place, but in some cases there were minor differences in such things as brackets, as the ideal positions and shapes were worked out in the light of experience. It would be pointless here to attempt to list every variation encountered on a pre-production chassis, because every pre-production Land Rover was a work in progress, and evolved over time as improvements were tried and adopted. However, it is possible to highlight a few common features – not least because, as the next chapter explains, many early production vehicles were built with chassis that had clearly been made to pre-production designs.

The pre-production chassis were all galvanised, which was considered the most effective way of guarding against corrosion. However, this proved expensive and time-consuming, and as a result the silver finish on early production chassis was not galvanised but painted.

Several early models were built with a front bumper that was welded to the chassis, but replacement proved difficult if the bumper was damaged, and a bolt-on design was ready before the Amsterdam Show and was displayed there. The pre-production chassis did not originally have a guard for the under-seat fuel tank, which no doubt resulted in damage during rough off-road use. They also had bulkhead outriggers

Pre-production front springs had squared ends. These were carried over onto early production models before being replaced by a design with rounded ends in late 1948.

that tapered in plan view, instead of the rectangular shape of the production type, and there were several differences in the body mounting arrangements. There were, for example, additional holes in the rear cross-member to aid fitting of the body, and the seat box mountings on the side rails were

THE CENTRE-STEER

It is probably as well to deal with some of the myths surrounding the legendary Centre-Steer model. This was what we would today call a "mule" – an existing vehicle modified to incorporate elements intended for a new one in order to act as a rolling test-bed.

Not quite the real thing, but a faithful reproduction of the legendary Centre-Steer model that was built by Bill Hayfield. It now belongs to the famous Dunsfold Collection of Land Rovers.

The driver had to sit astride the transmission tunnel, with the clutch pedal on the left and the brake and accelerator on the right.

Rover's Chief Engineer Maurice Wilks had it built on the chassis of a demobbed wartime Jeep while his designers were drawing up the vehicle that would become the real Land Rover. It appears that Wilks had already tried out the new Rover engine in a Jeep, and that the legendary Centre-Steer may have been a further development of that same vehicle. One way or the other, it had a new body that was built by hand in the Jig Shop at Solihull to give a rough idea of what the Land Rover might look like. It had a Rover engine – probably a redundant prototype of a smaller-capacity IOE type than the one that entered production in 1948 – and it had a Rover gearbox and axles, with a transfer box added into the driveline to give drive to both axles and to change from tall gearing for road work to crawler ratios for off-road work.

It also had its steering wheel in the middle, linked by chain to the original Jeep steering box on the left of the chassis. There have been several theories about this. Some people have argued that Wilks intended the Land Rover as an agricultural vehicle and, as agricultural tractors had a central driving position, a similar position would add to the Land Rover's appeal. Much more likely is that he hoped a central steering position would remove the complication of having both left-hand-drive and right-hand-drive variants in production on the same assembly lines.

The result did not impress his engineers. Arthur Goddard, who was running the Land Rover development programme, dismissed the vehicle more or less out of hand, and Tom Barton (later the top Land Rover engineer but at this stage still very junior) remembered that it was impractical because, with the hood up, following drivers could not see the hand signals that were very common in the days before flashing direction indicators.

Did more than one Centre-Steer exist? It is highly unlikely that there was more than one. This single "mule" appeared in September 1947 and allowed some testing of ideas and components over the next three months or so, but during January 1948 the first of the properly designed pre-production Land Rovers was completed, and the focus immediately shifted on to these. Maurice Wilks' son, Stephen, remembered his father showing him a pile of parts in the factory and saying that this was all that remained of the Centre-Steer. So there is little point in believing that it survives.

Not that this has prevented some highly motivated individuals from creating replicas from the few photographs that exist. As replicas, however good, they are of course beyond the scope of this book.

The early exhaust system, seen here on R14, used the long tubular silencer from the contemporary Rover P3 saloon car.

The early fuel tank, again seen on R14, had no undershield. It also had a galvanised finish instead of the later plated type.

square rather than the round type used on production.

As originally built, 26 of the pre-production chassis had right-hand drive and 22 had left-hand drive, but at least seven of the LHD chassis were converted to RHD at some point in their lives. This would have been done mainly to provide enough of the right type for testing; it was quicker than waiting for another vehicle to be built.

Engine

The pre-production engine was the 1.6-litre IOE four-cylinder that was also used for the first production models. On the early examples, there was a different exhaust system. This had a short front downpipe that led to a long tubular silencer (from the Rover P3 saloon car) mounted outside the chassis rail. This led to a pipe that discharged below the rear cross-member on the left-hand side. The production system with its tailpipe emerging from the rear silencer on the right-hand side of the vehicle was developed on these models, and later examples of the pre-production batch were built with this.

Transmission

The earliest pre-production models were built with a permanent four-wheel drive system and a freewheel, as would be used on the first production models. Several later ones were built with, or modified to have, a selectable four-wheel drive system that required extra controls.

In the beginning, these controls were designed as rods that emerged through the bulkhead below the instrument panel, but these proved difficult to use and were probably deleted from the specification before the 20th vehicle had been built. Subsequent models had the simplified controls that were used on production when selectable four-wheel drive replaced the original system in October 1950.

Some pre-production models had both a freewheel control and a selectable four-wheel drive system, and R16 was one of them. Its freewheel control lever was later removed, but the redundant selector remained in place on the front of the freewheel housing (and is the black item shown here). (Peter Galilee)

Early pre-production models had these rod-type transmission controls in the bulkhead, but they proved impractical and were changed. Note also the curious shape of the gear lever on this one, pictured while under construction in 1948.

The Land Rover logo had not been settled when the pre-production models were built, and they therefore had a plain grille without one. Note here the identification number painted on the front cross-member (white in this case) and the welded bumper.

Pre-production models had this flimsy hinge arrangement for the detachable door tops. A stronger design was developed for production.

The "gate-latch" door releases readily snagged clothing, and may have proved fragile as well.

Production spare wheel supports were a single pressing, but on the pre-production models they were fabricated. The weld line is visible where the flange meets the domed section.

Body

It was always the plan that the Land Rover bodies should be made of an alloy that was easier to work than steel and was corrosion resistant. The alloy used for the pre-production models was 12swg Duralumin, which was thicker and harder to work than the 16swg Birmabright chosen for production. Where steel was used for the body cappings, it was always galvanised, but the bulkhead was left untreated.

Other early features bore witness to the fact that the design was still being developed. Many pre-production models had wood packing to make their bodies fit properly to the chassis at the rear. Playing for safety, Rover designed the tailboard with three external vertical braces. This proved to be overkill, and just one vertical brace was used on production models. The lid for the petrol tank locker was smaller than the production type and was pear-shaped. The windscreen

Seen on R14, this is the pre-production style of tailboard with three vertical strengthening ribs. Also clear in this picture is the wood packing between body and rear cross-member.

The pre-production bulkhead had an angular top, as seen here.

Pre-production hoods had brass loops for the attachment to the windscreen header rail.

frame was different, too, with a wider vertical bar than on production types (although this was retained for early production models) and larger-diameter aluminium sockets for the hood sticks, with wing nuts securing them to small brackets on the windscreen frame.

Early pre-production vehicles had a rubber buffer mounted to each door instead of in the later position on the front wing. They also had a door release that projected above the door and had a T-shaped grip. This was abandoned either because it was prone to catch on clothes or because it proved too fragile. Pre-production sidescreens had a simple piece of bent wire to act as a hinge. Other features included smaller rivets than the production type, and a two-piece spare wheel mount that was welded together instead of the single-piece pressing developed for production.

The paint colour also changed while these vehicles were being built. The first pre-production models were painted in aircraft Cockpit Green, of which supplies were probably

Many pre-production models were fitted with parts that had been fabricated, as the production tooling had not yet been made. These bronze pedals are typical.

plentiful after the war. However, when the new Rover P3 60 and 75 saloons became available in February 1948, one of their colour options was a very similar shade that Rover knew as "No2 Green" (it was simply the second colour in the list of options). So after about 40 Land Rovers had been built, this slightly darker colour was standardised, no doubt to simplify production logistics and reduce costs.

Interior

Among the features that were developed on the pre-production models were the transmission controls, as explained above. There was also work on the position and type of the starter button, but all the known survivors of the batch were fitted with the production type before they left Rover Company ownership.

Inevitably, there were also some hand-fabricated items for the simple reason that no production tooling had yet been made. For example, the early pre-production Land Rovers had bronze pedals because Rover could not afford to wait until tooling was available for making steel ones.

The backrest of each seat was a curved horizontal metal bar that was bolted to the capping on the forward edge of the body tub by means of two short brackets with angled flanges. This bar was about four inches deep, and was padded and covered with Vynide. The seat cushions, also covered in Vynide, were flat and not very supportive. At least some pre-production seat backs and cushions were probably black rather than green, which became the standard colour.

Further developments

From the beginning, Maurice Wilks envisaged the Land Rover as a basic platform from which other variants could be developed. Some of these were tried out on the pre-production models. One plan was for a seven-seat Station Wagon, and in fact two chassis were appropriately converted; one (L20) became the first Land Rover to be bodied by Tickford and thus the forerunner of the production design, and the other (R02) had a rather less refined design that may have been in part an exercise to see whether Rover could do the job themselves more cheaply.

There were also plans for a mobile welder, and L05 was equipped as the prototype before going on display at the Amsterdam Show at the end of April 1948. A rural or factory fire engine was on the agenda, too, and R06 was converted to a prototype specification that would eventually give rise to a catalogued model.

Another pre-production characteristic is the weld line on the steering column support seen here.

CHASSIS, AXLES, SUSPENSION, STEERING, BRAKES, WHEELS & TYRES

CHASSIS FRAME

The Land Rover's chassis was always a ladder-frame type, manufactured from 14swg steel. It was deliberately rugged and deliberately simple in design, the latter so that it could be made by hand without the need for press tooling. There was a queue for new press tooling in the years immediately after the war, and Rover could not afford to wait.

The chassis frame consisted of box-section side rails with five box-section cross-members; the original plan was for the front bumper to be an integral part of the chassis, and so Rover literature often described this as "no 1 cross-member" – so making the total up to six. The basic ladder-frame was supplemented by four outriggers to support the body and by one to support the fuel tank.

The major box-section elements were assembled in a jig, using four flat pieces of steel that were seam-welded together along their edges. The theory was that any distortion in one panel would be corrected when it was welded to the others, and that theory held good. The chassis frames were deliberately not handed to suit either left-hand or right-hand drive, with the result that there were (for example) two positions for a steering relay. The redundant one was simply not used in the beginning, but from late 1948 or early 1949 it was blanked off as well.

Dumb irons

As noted above, the front bumper was an integral part of the chassis frame in the original design, and was therefore welded to the dumb irons on the pre-production models. However, this made repair and replacement difficult, and so on production the bumper was made detachable.

On models built until some point in 1949, there were fishplate brackets welded to the dumb irons, and these brackets had bolt holes for the front bumper fixings. With effect from chassis number 0610-3841 in November 1949, the dumb irons were simply drilled to receive bolts, and attachment brackets were mounted on the front bumper instead. This is the change point shown in the Parts Catalogue, but there are different opinions about its timing; see the section on the Bumper, below.

The chassis was always a ladder-frame type with welded box-section members. This one was pictured under restoration and belongs to 1948 Land Rover R86-0027, one of the oldest known survivors.

Front end

Just above the no 2 cross-member on the right-hand side of the chassis frame was a flat battery support platform on four short "legs". A frame to support the battery was bolted to this, and on its rear face carried a support plate for the air cleaner.

There were early and late types of battery support. The early one had deep walls and a detachable side-plate that was held in position by wing-nuts, and there were two sponge strips to help grip the battery and to prevent it from sliding about. The air cleaner support plate was attached to the battery support assembly and had three toggle clamps to hold the air cleaner itself in position.

In November 1950, at the same time as the transmission changed from the freewheel type to the selectable four-wheel-drive type, the battery support was changed. This later type had shallow sides, with a removable upper frame that sat on the top of the battery itself and was attached to the lower support by three vertical rods with brass wing nuts on their

This is the early battery platform. Also clear in this picture of a right-hand-drive model are the top mounting for the front damper, the run of the brake pipe, and the steering relay.

Early details (1): on the earliest chassis, the square body mounting plate was carried over from the pre-production models. Later production models had a round plate.

Early details (2): the bulkhead outriggers were gently tapered on pre-production and very early chassis. They were subsequently changed for a straight-edged type.

threaded top ends. The air cleaner was then held in place by a metal strap that ran up from the support plate and over the top of the unit. This change took place (at least theoretically) at chassis numbers 1610-0603, 1613-1573, 1616-0909, 1663-0025 and 1666-0787.

All chassis have tubes welded into the appropriate side member to take the pedal cross-tubes. On very early chassis – perhaps no more than the first 20 or so – the chassis were for universal use and these tubes were fitted in both side rails rather than only the one on the driver's side.

The first 1500 chassis have two guide tubes in each chassis side rail for the bulkhead fixings. It appears that the triangular supports on the bulkhead through which the fixing bolts passed were not pre-drilled, but were drilled to accept the bolts after the bulkhead had been lined up on the assembly track. This is one reason why the bulkhead from one vehicle may not seem to line up correctly on another one; there were minor variations in the position of the drilled holes.

Bumper

All production 80-inch Land Rovers had a detachable front bumper, and on the earliest models this was galvanised to improve its durability. However, after about 150-200 vehicles had been built, it was simply painted silver rather than galvanised, probably as a cost-saving measure. Making the bumper detachable increased the overall length of the vehicle by around three inches as compared to the pre-production specification with its integral welded bumper. All bumpers had a small aperture for the starting-handle to pass through, with a diamond-shaped reinforcing plate across it.

Early bumpers were drilled to accept bolts that passed through the fishplates on the front dumb-irons and were

Early details (3): chassis R86-0027 shows the early body mounting arrangement on the rear cross-member. The securing bolt passed through the hole in the top face, and the larger hole in the bottom face provided access to the bolt head.

secured by nuts and washers below the bumper. In the beginning, the back of the bumper was open along its full length, but on later ones the ends were boxed in.

During the 1950 season, the fishplates were deleted from the front dumb-irons and shorter support brackets were welded to the bumper instead. This may well have been intended to reduce repair costs. In other respects, these bumpers were unchanged from the early type with boxed-in ends. There are unreconciled opinions on when this change took place. The Rover Parts Book gives the changeover point as chassis number 0610-3840 during the 1950 season, but some experts believe that the change had actually taken place some months earlier at 866-6000 in summer 1949 and that old stock was used up over the next few months.

This is a "fishplate" chassis; the front bumper was bolted between the two plates welded to the front dumb-iron.

Front (no 2) cross-member

Working back from the bumper, the no 2 or front cross-member is the first proper cross-member on the chassis frame. It always had a circular aperture to allow the starting-handle to pass through, and either one or two apertures for the steering mechanism.

There were three stages in the development of this cross-member. On the first 150 or so chassis, it was fabricated and the tube for the starting-handle stood slightly proud of the front face. These chassis could be built up with either LHD or RHD, and there was a vertical tube welded on both the left and right sides, to take the steering relay. The cross-member was subsequently pressed (which saved costs), and Rover tidied up its appearance by ensuring that the ends of the starting-handle tube were finished off flush with its front and rear faces.

The bumper is in place here on a "fishplate" chassis from August 1949.

The third stage probably arrived at about the same time as chassis changed from silver to green (ie after about 4500 had been built). In this case, only one vertical tube for the steering relay was welded in place, and the redundant position was filled with a circular plate.

Engine (no 3) cross-member

The cross-member below the engine had solid faces without apertures.

Gearbox (no 4) cross-member

This was bolted to the underside of the side rails, with two bolts on either side, so that it could be removed for work on the transmission. Very early ones were not fully boxed, but this cross-member was boxed-in after probably fewer than 100 vehicles had been built, to improve protection for the transmission from grounding.

Front body support (no 5) cross-member

The no 5 cross-member was welded in place and provided support for the front end of the body tub. There were two vertical brackets welded to this cross-member to which the

This late 1949 chassis shows the later type of bumper fixing, where brackets on the bumper itself replaced the fishplates on the chassis.

The early drawbar had ten holes in its horizontal face.

body would be bolted.

This cross-member had a circular cut-out to allow a driveshaft for the rear PTO (when fitted) to pass through. As on other cross-members with similar apertures, the lining tube initially protruded a little beyond the face of the cross-member, but the finish was tidied up in late 1948 or early 1949.

On the 1952 and 1953 chassis, two transverse bracings were added to the chassis between the no 5 and no 6 cross-members to give more support to the floor of the body tub.

Rear (no 6) cross-member

The rear cross-member was welded in place across the rear of the side rails. It was wider than the intermediate cross-members, extending beyond the side rails to line up with the outriggers. It also had a tunnel for a PTO shaft, and this was made neater in late 1948 or early 1949 in the same way as others. Very early cross-members had channel-section ends, but these were boxed in from quite early on.

The functions of the rear cross-member were to strengthen the chassis at the rear and to support the rear end of the body tub. It always had four vertical brackets, to which the body tub would be bolted.

There was a lifting handle bolted to each end of the rear cross-member. These were for de-ditching purposes (an idea carried over from the Jeep) and also served to protect the rear corners of the vehicle from minor damage. All had a galvanised finish and all were bolted through the rear face of the cross-member by four bolts. There is clear evidence that a shortage of these handles occurred after about 100 chassis had been built, and that perhaps as many as another 100 were shipped off to dealers without them. In these cases, the fixing bolts were simply bolted in place to fill the pre-drilled holes in the cross-member.

Early lifting handles had a flattened section between the curved handle and the flat fixing bracket; later ones did not. It is generally accepted that the changeover took place during the 1949 season, and it is also clear that some vehicles built around this time had a mixture of both types from new.

A pre-wired towing plug was let into the right-hand side of the rear cross-member as standard, and from May 1949 cross-members had four holes for the fixing bracket bolts around the hole for the trailer plug. For more detail on this, please see the Electrical section.

Drawbar

A drawbar (towing plate) was normally mounted to the bottom of the rear cross-member on early models. This step-like structure had ten holes in its horizontal surface and was welded in place.

When the big order for Land Rovers arrived from the British military in summer 1949, it came with a request to delete the drawbar, which did restrict the departure angle of the vehicle. Rover obliged, but for civilian models from 0610-3841 in November 1949 specified a new design of drawbar that had only eight holes in its horizontal surface and was bolted rather than welded in place. This change coincided with the change to the front bumper that saw its mounting brackets transferred from the dumb irons to the bumper itself.

There are different opinions about how long the drawbar remained a standard fitting; some commentators suggest that it was deleted in 1949 at the same time as the bumper fishplates were deleted from the front of the chassis, but others believe it was fitted until the end of 0610-series (1950 model) production. The truth may lie somewhere between the two opinions, and it may be that the drawbar was added or not fitted to suit local market requirements or a customer's preference.

Outriggers

All chassis had two box-section outriggers on each side, welded outboard of the side rails. Their function was to support the body. There was one just ahead of the gearbox cross-member on each side, to which the bulkhead was bolted; on the first 150 or so vehicles, these outriggers were noticeably squarer in appearance than later ones. The second outrigger on each side was alongside the no 5 or front body support cross-member.

On the right-hand side of the chassis frame, there was an additional outrigger between the engine and gearbox cross-members, again welded to the outside of the side rail. This served as a front mounting support for the fuel tank.

Finish

Production 80-inch chassis were always painted. Only the pre-production chassis were galvanised, although the myth still persists that all early Land Rover chassis had this treatment. (Nevertheless, many reproduction chassis have been galvanised for long life, and that can only be a good thing.)

The first 4500 chassis were painted silver, to resemble the galvanised finish of the pre-production models. In approximately May 1949, the chassis colour was changed to Light Green to match the bodywork. There were then around 1500 vehicles with this chassis colour before the chassis paint changed to Dark Green to match a similar change for the bodywork. This change took place at approximately chassis number 866-6000.

All subsequent 80-inch chassis were painted in the body colour – or, in the case of vehicles painted in a customer's livery, in whatever was the standard production chassis colour at the time. (Those delivered to the Royal Air Force nevertheless all seem to have had RAF Blue chassis.)

Brackets and check straps

Spring-hanger brackets were welded to the lower section of each chassis rail, two for each front spring and two for each rear spring. The shape of the brackets for the front springs changed when the spring shackles moved from the front to the rear of the springs in June 1950. On pre-production models, the front spring shackles had a "pointed" shape to the metal around the bolt holes, and this type was used up on early production chassis up to about number 150. The ends of the shackles were then rounded off.

On early models, the attachment pins for the top fixing eyes of the four dampers were welded to the side rails of the chassis. These were difficult to repair when they broke, which appears to have been often enough to cause concern. So at 0610-0156 in July 1949 they were replaced by a bracket welded to the chassis that was drilled to accept a long bolt instead of the fixed pin. This design stood the test of time, although the "saddle" sections of the bracket that fitted over the chassis rail were modified at an unknown point (chassis 0610-3841 has been suggested) before 1951.

There was also a U-shaped check strap for the rear axle attached to each side rail; its purpose was to restrict downward movement of the axle in extreme conditions. The check straps were made of khaki webbing, with a rectangular steel plate at each end. Two set bolts passed through each end of the webbing and its steel plate, and into threaded plates welded to the side rails above the rear axle. Early vehicles with the long-nose differential (see Axles, below) had longer check straps than the later ones with the short-nose differential.

There were four rubber bump-stops for the axles, each one bolted to the lower face of the chassis side rail. Front and rear types were different, and wider front ones were specified to go with the wider 2½-inch road springs when these were fitted

Up to June 1950, there were swinging shackles at the leading edge of each front spring.

Restored, and with the spring mounting bush in pace, this is the front shackle mounting on R86-0027.

Pictured on a restored 1953 2-litre chassis, this is the front mounting for the front road spring. The yellow paint is not standard; this vehicle was new to the Automobile Association.

FACTORY-ORIGINAL LAND ROVER SERIES 1, 80-INCH MODELS

This is the swinging shackle at the rear of a front spring on the 1953 2-litre chassis.

The additional chassis bracing for the load area is seen here on a 1952 military instructional chassis.

AXLES

Axle casings and differential casings were always finished in black unless to special order. Axles are often described by the type of differential fitted, whether short-nose or long-nose; for an explanation, see the section on Differentials below.

Front axles

There were design differences between axles for LHD vehicles and those for RHD vehicles because of differences in the steering linkages. The two types are clearly identifiable by means of their prefix numbers (see the table opposite).

The design of the front axle casing changed in approximately July 1950, when 2½in wide road springs replaced the earlier 1¾in wide type. The later ones – beginning with axle number 0611-4001 – have wider spring seats to suit. Early front axles have fixed steering lock stops, but from November 1948 adjustable stops were made standard, probably to suit the introduction of the wider 7.00x16 tyre option.

The half-shafts – one short and one long to suit the offset differential – are each divided into two by a Tracta joint that allows the drive to be transmitted while the angle of the drive-shaft is changed through the steering mechanism. (In practice, many vehicles will have had the early Tracta-type half-shafts replaced by Hardy Spicer types with more durable joints.) Each drive-shaft is attached to a hub assembly, and the road wheel is in turn bolted to this. At each end of the axle is a chromed spherical housing (familiarly known as a ball swivel), with its outer end partially covered by the swivel pin housing. On top of this second housing, the upper swivel pin is in unit with the steering lever; the lower swivel pin is fixed. The swivel pin housings initially had no drain plugs, but later

The air cleaner bracket was attached to the battery tray on later models like this 1953 2-litre. The sheathed cable runs to the choke knob and will later be attached to the carburettor.

from June 1950. For the 1952 models, wider bump stops were fitted to the rear as well, to match those at the front.

For the 1952 and 1953 chassis, two support angles were added to the rear of the chassis below the body tub. From May 1955, the replacement chassis frames that Rover supplied for the 1950 and later models were a composite type which had these angles; they could be removed if the chassis was used for a 1950 or 1951 model. Service literature suggested that these replacement chassis were suitable only for vehicles numbered from 0611-3530, 0620-0410 (Station Wagon) and 0630-0031 (Welder).

CHASSIS, AXLES, SUSPENSION, STEERING, BRAKES, WHEELS & TYRES

AXLE NUMBERS 1948-1953

Identifying numbers for all axles are stamped on top of the axle casing adjacent to the axle breather.

Note that these tables separate prefix from serial number with a dash to aid clarity. This dash is not found on the axles themselves.

Commencing numbers only are shown.

1948 and 1949 models
Front axle   86-0001   (with L prefix for LHD)
Rear axle   86-0001

1950 models
Front axle   0610-0001   (with L prefix for LHD)
                0611-0001
Rear axle   0610-0001
                0611-0001

1951 models
Front axle   1610-0001(RHD) 1613-0001 (LHD)
Rear axle   1610-0001

1952 models
Front axle   2610-0001 (RHD) 2613-0001 (LHD)
Rear axle   1610-0001

1953 models
Front axle   3610-0001 (RHD) 3613-0001 (LHD)
Rear axle   3610-0001

This drawing dates from January 1948 when the Land Rover was in its later design stages. The initials "RS" at the bottom right are those of Roland Seale, Rover's Chief Draughtsman.

This fully reconditioned front axle has the long-nose differential. The axle number – 860824 – can be clearly seen next to the breather and reveals that the differential has the early 4.88:1 gearing.

examples did have these.

Early Land Rovers had taper roller bearings on both upper and lower swivel pins, with shim adjustment. When attempts to cure wheel wobble by changes to the steering relay (see below) were not successful, Rover turned their attention to the upper swivel pins. They replaced the taper bearings with cone damper bearings; the lower swivel pins meanwhile remained unchanged. Some sources quote the change point as March 1950 and axles numbered 0611-3205 (RHD) and 0611-3116 (LHD); others show it as chassis number 0611-2001 in May 1950. It was possible to modify existing axles to the new standard, and probably many were updated to the later specification. In practice, Rover discovered soon afterwards that the major cause of wheel wobble lay in the front spring mountings, and made an appropriate modification (see Suspension, below).

There was a further modification to the cone damper bearings in late 1952 at axles numbered 2610-8221 and 2613-3681. In this case, the cones were modified to improve the oil

During production of the long-nose differentials, the rim of the casing was modified to incorporate some thicker sections, as seen on the example nearer the camera here. (Peter Galilee)

feed to the bearings, and now had a vertical hole and four radial drillings. It was possible to modify existing vehicles to the new standard.

After 80-inch production had ended, a rectangular section spring was added to the swivel pins on 86-inch and 107-inch models, again to help improve damping of the steering. This modification was made on production in approximately February 1954, and could also be made retrospectively to 80-inch models with front axles numbered from 0611-3205 (RHD) and 0611-3116 (LHD) onwards; that is, those with the later cone damper bearings.

Rear axles

The rear axle was always a semi-floating type, and the axle casing was the same on all 80-inch models.

The front differential in place on a 1953 2-litre model. Visible just outboard of the axle breather is the axle number, commencing 3610.

There were two types of half-shaft, and the difference is easily visible in the ends that are visible through the wheel centres. There were actually three different types of these, but the first type was used only on the first 150 or so vehicles. It has a thick flange, a flat dish and (invisibly unless the half-shaft has been withdrawn) a bolt-on dust cover behind the driving flange.

The second type has a thin flange and a flat dish, and there is a tin dust cover that is hammered into place behind the driving flange. The third type was introduced at axle number 86-7721 with the later type of half-shaft, around the middle of the 1949 season. The end of the half-shaft has a thin flange with a double-dished end, and the dust cover behind is pressed and peened over.

All half-shaft ends have a black chemical finish and trying to replicate this with black paint can cause problems. Paint tends to block the drilled holes that allow oil to drain onto the wheel's nave plate if an oil seal fails, and if that oil is unable to escape as intended, it drains onto the brakes.

Differentials

There were three major types of differential, all with spiral bevel gears. The earliest ones are long-nose types, with a 4.88:1 gearset, and these are the same as the ones used in the last of the 1947-model Rover saloons. They were probably used until approximately September 1948.

By this stage, the Rover P3 saloons had replaced the 1947 models, and they had a 4.7:1 differential gearset. So this was used, in the long-nose casing, but it became a temporary and transitional specification.

The third type of differential retained the latest 4.7:1 gearing, but had a noticeably shorter nose-piece, which had been designed because the long-nose types caused problems with propshaft operating angles.

Rover Service literature suggests that the 4.7:1 ratio was introduced at front and rear axles numbered 86-1320, which it also claims coincided with chassis number 86-1001 in December 1948. (An earlier handbook that claimed the first 4.7:1 axle was numbered 86-1372 may have been predicting a change that had not yet occurred.) Expert opinion is that the chassis number associated with the change may have been 200 or so higher than the one quoted. A surviving document shows that this change was planned as early as January 1948: there were to be 1050 axle sets with the 4.88 ratio, which can be interpreted as 50 pre-production and 1000 production models.

There was a minor variation during production of the long-nose differentials, where the cast rim of the differential casing on later examples had thicker sections at intervals, presumably to increase its strength.

There were also some variations early in the life of the short-nose differentials. The early ones have the circular drive flange that was used on the P3 saloons, but the later ones

CHASSIS, AXLES, SUSPENSION, STEERING, BRAKES, WHEELS & TYRES

This underside view shows an 0610-series chassis with the narrow front springs that had their shackles at the front ends.

(from axle 0610-6001) have the square drive flange that was introduced on the P4 saloons in September 1949, plus minor differences in the crown wheel and pinion assemblies. From the start of 1951 production (so, on axles with 161-, 261- and 361- prefixes), spring washers were added to all 10 bolts that hold the differential casing to the axle casing.

Suspension

All 80-inch Land Rover springs were semi-elliptic leaf types, and all dampers were telescopic.

There were some minor variations in the spring shackle fixings. Up to and including chassis 86-0647 in November 1948, all shackle pins were the same. However, from 86-0648 the inner spring mounting points were no longer tapped, and so four of the pins had less thread than before and were designed as a tight push-fit into the chassis. A second change took place in May 1949 at chassis 866-5465, when the washers initially fitted between the front spring bushes and the shackle plates were deleted.

Front springs

The front road springs were never handed, but there were several different specifications. All the early springs had a width of 1¾in and were shackled at the front, but from mid-1950 new springs were fitted with a 2½in width and the shackles at the rear. Springs all had a black heat-treated finish, and are not handed; however, the different types of springs are not interchangeable.

The earliest front springs were eight-leaf types, with a free

A front bump-stop in place on an early silver chassis.

This is the rear bump-stop. The two black plates on the chassis rail will hold the webbing axle strap when this has been fitted.

camber of 2.5in (63.5mm) and 3 inches between the spring eye centre and the end of the third leaf. These were fitted on chassis up to and including 86-0525 in early November 1948. The springs were then changed to eight-leaf types with a free camber of 3.3 inches (89mm) and 1.25 inches between the spring eye centre and the end of third leaf. Both these types had a square section on the second leaf where it wrapped around the spring eye and back on top of the first leaf. Original versions also had clamps with a bolt that passed over the top leaf.

These early eight-leaf springs tended to flatten out in use, and from chassis 86-2115 in January 1949, new springs with nine leaves were fitted. These had 4 inches of free camber and could be identified by different clamps, which had no bolt but were simply turned inwards over the main leaf. Their second leaf also curved around the spring eye and back onto the main leaf.

For both of the early types, Rover provided a special service replacement spring, with nine leaves, 3.5 inches of free camber, and all the spring clips turned over the main leaf. It was also possible to modify the eight-leaf types to a nine-leaf configuration by dismantling them and adding an extra leaf.

The wheel wobble problem mentioned earlier (see Axles) was eventually traced to the shackled front ends of the springs. So Rover made several changes in June 1950, the most obvious being to turn the springs round so that their front ends were fixed and the rear ends were shackled. (It is not clear why this change was not recorded in Rover Service Bulletins at the time.) At the same time, wider springs were fitted, with a 2½in width instead of the earlier 1¾in size, and these were accompanied by dampers to a new specification, and wider bump-stops. This final type of "wide" spring was fitted from chassis number 0611-3530 on basic models.

Rear springs

Rear springs always had the same black heat-treated finish as the front springs. Although the first 2297 Land Rovers had the same springs on both sides at the rear, handed springs were then introduced to compensate for extra weight on the right of the chassis. This came mainly from the fuel tank (and not from the driver – otherwise there would have had to be differences between LHD and RHD specifications).

The specification of the earliest springs is of academic interest only because these were no longer supplied as service replacements after May 1949. However, it is included here for the sake of completeness. Up to chassis number 86-2297, both left-hand and right-hand rear springs had the same 4 3/8in free camber. At that point, handed springs were introduced, and these were identified by stampings "LH" or "RH" as appropriate. The left-hand spring had the original 4 3/8in free camber, but the right-hand one had 5 inches of free camber.

From chassis 866-4116, the camber of the springs was reduced to reduce the normal operating angle of the rear propshaft. Those on the left (stamped LH) had 4 inches of free camber, and those on the right (stamped RH) had 4.5 inches of free camber.

The only further change worth noting took place in February 1949, when a shield plate was fitted to the left-hand spring between the check strap and the brake pipe, to prevent the slack strap chafing on the pipe. It was attached to the spring dowel, at the outboard front end of the axle tube.

There was also a heavy-duty rear spring option (see Optional Equipment).

Dampers

Original equipment dampers were Woodhead Monroe telescopics all round.

Early front dampers had a compressed length of 11 7/8in (302mm) and an extended length of 17 7/8in (454mm), and these were used with the eight-leaf springs up to and including chassis number 86-2114. With the nine-leaf springs, the front dampers were changed to the slightly longer type already in use at the rear (see below). This second type was then used up to chassis number 0611-3529. Both early types were code-marked 1T8-4.

Thereafter, front dampers with the same compressed and extended lengths as before but with a different specification were fitted (these later ones had a code marking of 3T8-B1 and a yellow paint identification).

At the rear, the dampers initially had a compressed length of 13 5/16in (335mm) and an extended length of 20 7/16in (519mm). These were code marked 1T8-C4, and were used up to chassis number 0611-3529 – the same point at which the front dampers changed. They then changed to a new type with the same compressed and extended lengths. These were code-marked 4T8-A6 and had green paint identification.

Brakes

Original braking equipment on the 80-inch models was always made by Girling. There were hydraulically-operated drums on the road wheels and a mechanically-operated drum for the parking brake, which was mounted on the transfer box output shaft.

Wheel brakes

The brake drums on the road wheels always had a 10-inch diameter, and were leading-and-trailing-shoe types with 1½in wide shoes. Back plates and drums originally had a semi-gloss black finish.

Two major types of brake were used, early ones being self-adjusting to compensate for wear (Girling Hydrastatic), and the later ones having manual adjustment. The change was probably made because the Hydrastatic brakes wore their shoes out more quickly. The drums were the same on both types, but the later type had different backplates with an extra

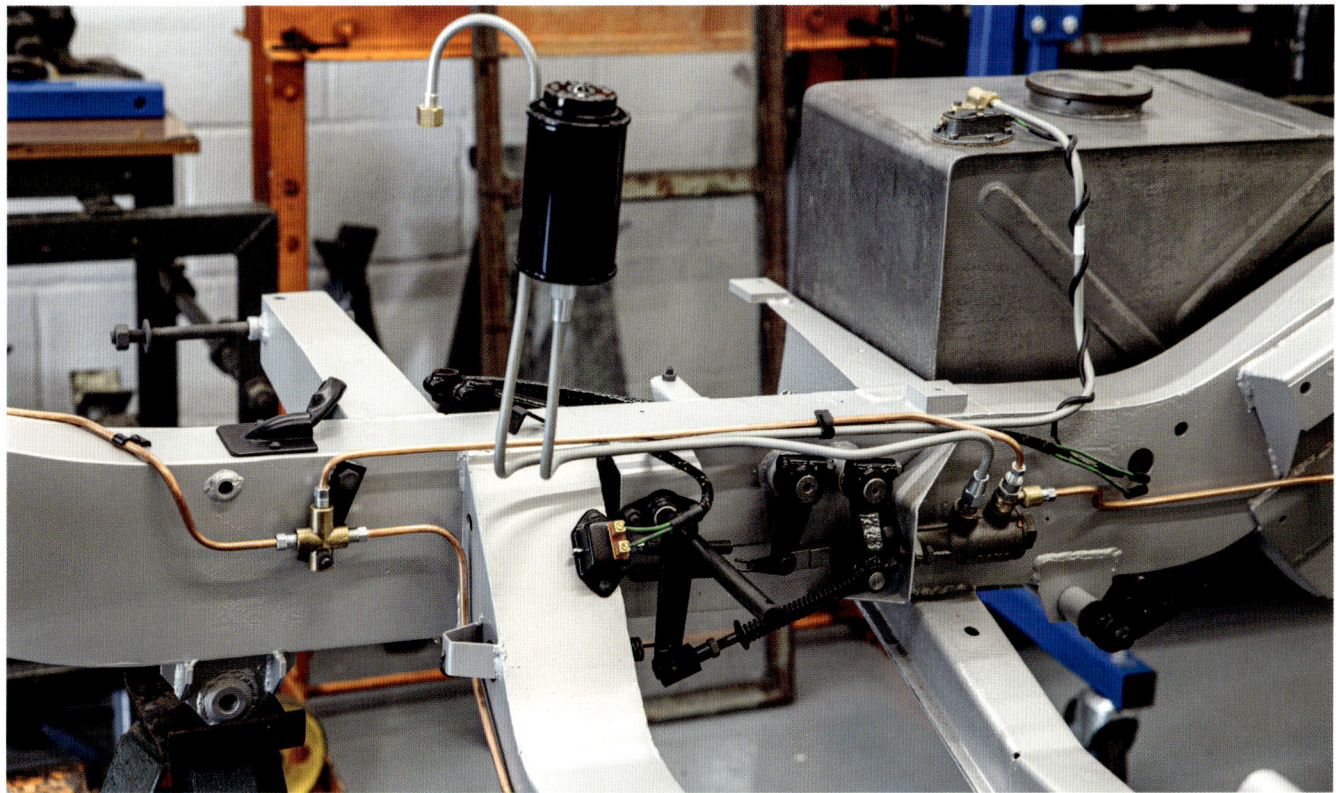

Multiple points of detail are visible in this picture of chassis R86-0027 under restoration. Note the position of the fluid reservoir, the brake pipes, and the elements of the clutch operating mechanism.

spring between the leading shoe and a post on the backplate, and a snail cam adjuster. It was possible to buy a kit of parts to convert a vehicle from the early to the later type of brakes.

The change was announced in the March 1950 Service Bulletin, which claimed that the changeover point was at chassis 866-7575 (which was completed in July 1949). This number was confirmed in the December 1949 Workshop Manual, but the early date rather suggests that this was an intended changeover point and not necessarily the actual one. All the later Parts Catalogues put the change at axle number 866-7720, but of course surviving records do not tie axle numbers to chassis numbers.

Brake linings were initially either Ferodo MR41 or Don BS5 types. The Don type became the Service replacement. The later brakes had solid brake linings, but the Hydrastatic brakes had a cut through each lining.

Fluid reservoir and master cylinder

The brake fluid reservoir was always a black metal cylinder with a screw top. When new, these cylinders carried a blue decal with orange lettering that read, "Use only Genuine Girling Brake Fluid". Good reproductions have been made available.

On the first 1000 vehicles, the reservoir was located rather inaccessibly on the engine side of the bulkhead, on the inner wall of the driver's footwell. So from chassis number 86-1001, in early December 1948, it was relocated on a bracket welded to the chassis rail on the appropriate side. On right-hand-drive models, this was just inboard of the fuel tank, next to the handbrake mounting bracket, and on left-hand-drive models it was in the equivalent position on the opposite chassis rail. The pre-drilled mounting hole in the bulkhead footwell panel probably lasted beyond the changeover.

These are the pedal operating rods seen from the other side. Their cross-tubes run through the chassis side-rail.

The brake master cylinder was always a Girling CB type with an unpolished bare metal finish. It was located on the engine side of the bulkhead, above the pedal box.

Brake pipes and hoses

Original brake pipes were always made of steel and were unpainted (although many restored vehicles have been fitted with more durable modern pipes). They were held to the chassis frame by metal clips with a yellowish plated finish that were screwed in place. On the rear axle, the brake pipes were installed along the front of the axle and differential housing (although some restorers prefer to fit them in a less vulnerable position behind the axle).

There were flexible rubber hoses at each front wheel, and a third one running from the T-piece attached to the centre of the rear axle. All these hoses were originally black.

Transmission brake

The transmission brake had a 9in diameter and its backplate was the same on 80-inch Land Rovers of all ages. The drum (with the usual black finish) also seems to have been the same on all models, even though Parts Catalogues suggest that the one fitted to 2-litre models differed from the earlier type. The original equipment linings for the transmission brake were always Ferodo MR19 types.

There was a minor change to the handbrake mechanism at chassis 86-6000 in June 1949, but the changeover was not a clean one and old stock parts were used up over next few months.

A ball swivel and the adjustable lock-stop bolt are clear in this picture of a 1950 0610-series chassis.

Steering

All 80-inch Land Rovers had the same type of Burman Douglas worm and nut steering, with a 15:1 ratio that gives 2.4 turns of the steering wheel from lock to lock.

The steering box receives inputs from the steering column and transmits movement through a drop arm to a longitudinal rod that runs above the chassis rail on the same side to a relay on the no 2 chassis cross-member. The relay then operates a lever that moves a drag link connected to the wheel on the opposite side of the vehicle. The front wheels are kept parallel by an adjustable track rod that runs between them, and all moving connections use ball joints.

The steering box was mounted on the engine side of the bulkhead, on the left or the right side according to the steering position. Some steering boxes had a packing plate in the shape of a very thin wedge to give the correct alignment. The steering relay, all the rods and linkages, and the steering column were painted black. The ball joints all had a black chemical (not painted) finish, and there was a large black rubber shroud over the steering column where it passed through the bulkhead. This was intended to keep dust and fumes out of the driving compartment.

There was a modification to the steering column in April 1953, when a steel main nut and case-hardened inner column were fitted. The change occurred on the assembly lines at chassis numbers 3610-3422, 3613-3245, 3616-2792, 3663-3498, 3666-1341, 3630-0005, 3633-0005 and 3636-0003. The new parts could also be fitted to earlier vehicles, but only in sets.

Steering box

Early steering boxes were made of cast iron, and had an oil filler on the down tube. They were normally unpainted, although some experts believe very early ones may have had a black finish. The main shaft on these early boxes had a bronze nut with a steel insert, but the insert could pull out in service and so Burman changed the design to incorporate a steel nut with a coarser thread. It was possible to modify the early steering boxes to take the later steel nut. (Note that a very small number of vehicles had a cast bronze steering box that otherwise looks the same as the standard cast iron type. These steering boxes were probably pre-production items that were used up on assembly, and most have been found on vehicles built in early 1949.) Later steering boxes were cast from aluminium alloy, and had an oil filler on the casting. There were also a few transitional ones that had an aluminium alloy casing with both this filler and one on the down tube. All the alloy steering boxes are prone to cracking, typically around the top "collar" of the casting.

On the 1948-1951 models, there was a tendency for the bulkhead to crack around the steering box mounting. The modification prompted by this is described in the section on the Bulkhead, later.

CHASSIS, AXLES, SUSPENSION, STEERING, BRAKES, WHEELS & TYRES

Avon tyres were fitted to the earliest 80-inch models. This advertisement on the back cover of the October 1948 Operation Manual shows what their treads looked like. On the right, "for farm and road use" is the standard Avon Traction 6.00x16 size, and on the left, "for use on exceptionally soft surfaces" is the more aggressive Super Traction 7.00x16 tyre.

Dunlop Trakgrip tyres replaced the Avons on production, and an example is seen here. The sidewall carries clear identification, showing it is a T28 type with a 6.00x16 size.

Relay

As explained above, chassis were manufactured with a mounting position for the relay on each side. The redundant one was left exposed until late 1948 or early 1949 when it was blanked off.

Early steering relays had a single spring-loaded Tufnol cone, and an early attempt to cure wheel wobble was made around September 1948, when an inch-long packing piece was added to compress the spring in the relay; it was ultimately unsuccessful. A second attempt was made in January 1949 (at chassis 86-1901), when a double damping cone was fitted, and in April 1949 Rover dealers were sent revised relays to fit FOC to customer's existing vehicles. These later relays can be identified by four set screws holding the top and bottom covers and, unsurprisingly, very few original-pattern relays still survive. When this second change to the relay still did not solve the wheel wobble problem, Rover turned their attention to the swivel pins, and the modifications made to those have already been described in the section on Front Axles.

WHEELS AND TYRES
Wheels

All 80-inch Land Rovers had pressed steel disc wheels with a 16-inch diameter and five stud holes. They were painted to match the body colour. In the early days, Rover supplied balance weights (part number 230602), which had a screw fitting.

The earliest wheels had a 4½-inch rim width, with the hole for the tyre valve next to one of the slotted sections. These wheels were manufactured by Dunlop and were not dated. They were used up to chassis number 0610-2200 in late 1949.

A redesigned wheel with a 5-inch rim width was then introduced on production, and this was made readily distinguishable by a raised rim around the centre hole and by having the hole for the tyre valve in one of the "spokes" of the centre section. These later wheels were stamped with a date of manufacture, shown as a month above a year (eg 2 50 and 10 50 for February and October 1950 respectively).

Military-pattern split-rim wheels were also available as an option, and are described in the later section covering Optional Equipment. Some CKD models, notably those assembled in Australia, had locally-manufactured wheels (see Chapter 13).

41

FACTORY-ORIGINAL LAND ROVER SERIES 1, 80-INCH MODELS

Tyres

In the beginning, the standard tyre was an Avon Traction with a 6.00 x 16 size. The optional alternative was a 7.00 x 16 Super Traction, with a more aggressive tractor-type tread. Both types had a directional tread, and the V in the central part of the tread had to face the front of the vehicle. This arrangement was proved imperfect when the spare wheel had to be fitted, because sometimes the tyre would have been fitted to suit the opposite side of the vehicle, so that the V was facing the wrong way!

By October 1949, the Avon tyres had gone and Rover was fitting Dunlop Trakgrip types on the assembly lines, again with a directional tread. The standard type was a 6.00 x 16 Trakgrip T28, and the 7.00 x 16 option with more aggressive tread was a Trakgrip T25. The British Army, meanwhile, was using a Trakgrip T29 with a 6.50 x 16 size.

There were also two sand tyre options, and one or other of these would probably have been fitted as standard to vehicles destined for appropriate export territories. The more common type was a Dunlop Fort 7.00 x 16, but there was also a Dunlop Standard 7.00 x 16 for desert use. By the time of the 2-litre models that were introduced in autumn 1951, a Dunlop Fort in the smaller 6.00 x 16 size was also available.

This early wheel rim has lost most of its original No2 Green paint but shows clearly how the tyre valve was positioned between the "spokes" of the disc and between two of the fixing holes.

The later type of wheel rim has its tyre valve next to one of the wheel "spokes" and in line with one of the fixing lugs.

ENGINE, TRANSMISSION & EXHAUST

All the 80-inch models had a four-cylinder petrol engine with an inlet-over-exhaust valve layout. These engines were shared in their essentials with contemporary Rover saloon cars.

The engine was coupled to a four-speed gearbox with synchromesh on third and fourth gears only. This in turn drove through a transfer gearbox which took the drive to both front and rear axles via propshafts. The transfer gearbox provided two ranges of gears, the High range being for road work and the Low range for off-road use. There was also provision on the transfer gearbox for a power take-off that could be used when the vehicle was stationary.

ENGINE

The engine in the early 80-inch Land Rovers had a 1.6-litre (1595cc) swept volume and was similar to the one used in the Rover P3 60 saloon car of 1948-1949. It was quoted as delivering 50bhp at 4000rpm and 80 lb ft of torque at 2000rpm. Both figures were taken from bench tests and the real figures when installed in the vehicle were a little lower.

When it became clear that Land Rover customers would welcome more power and torque (mainly because they were asking more of their vehicles than Rover had anticipated), the engine was redesigned with a larger bore and a 2-litre (1997cc) swept volume. An experimental batch of these engines was made in 1950 and was tested extensively before production versions were made available in autumn 1951 for the 1952 models.

The 2-litre engines were claimed at the time to produce 58bhp at 2000rpm with 101 lb ft of torque at 1500rpm. The torque improvement was the more important one for most customers and in fact the power output was often subsequently quoted as just 52bhp, which was barely more than was available from the 1.6-litre engine.

Rover ceased to supply service exchange 1.6-litre engines for export customers in September 1952, although it appears that they remained available in Britain. When a 2-litre engine was supplied as a replacement for a 1.6-litre through the Rover Service Department, it came with a "conversion pack" of parts for which no charge was made. A Land Rover modified in this way may not be strictly original, but would have the benefit of a rather interesting history!

Factory reconditioned engines

Rover ran an engine reconditioning scheme, and from April 1957 that scheme underwent some revisions that were announced in the Service Bulletin for that month. So from that date, factory reconditioned engines were identified by a brass plate that was attached by screws to the cylinder block, next to the dipstick hole. The original engine number was completely removed from the block.

The brass plate showed the Rover Company name and had panels for two stamped numbers. The upper panel showed the engine part number, and the lower panel showed where the engine was reconditioned and indicated how it now differed from the standard specification. Engines were initially reconditioned at the factory in Solihull and at Rover's London Service Depot in Seagrave Road. From 1964 approximately,

A pair of fully rebuilt engines, seen here ready to go into vehicles. On the left, with the black oil filler-cum-breather tube, is the later 2-ltre type. The engine on the right, with the unpainted cast filler tube, is an early 1.6-litre.

FACTORY-ORIGINAL LAND ROVER SERIES 1, 80-INCH MODELS

The early 1.6-litre engines are known as "side-plate" types because of this feature. Note the simple hooked shape of the dipstick grip on this carefully rebuilt engine, which is early enough to feature the brass inlet manifold drain pipe.

THE 1.6-LITRE ENGINE

The 1.6-litre engine used in the Land Rover was related to but not the same as the one used in Rover cars. It was detuned to suit the low-quality fuel that Rover expected would be used in many export markets, with different pistons that gave a lower compression ratio (6.8:1 as against 7:1). It also had a different camshaft, which improved the low-speed torque delivery that was so important for a working vehicle. These engines all had an efficient wedge-shaped combustion chamber design, achieved by a sloping cylinder-block top face and an angled face on the head. The piston crowns were shaped to suit, and the overhead inlet valves were operated by pushrods while the exhaust valves were operated directly by the camshaft. This in turn was driven by a duplex roller chain from a pulley on the nose of the crankshaft.

Cylinder block, cylinder head & sump (1.6-litre)

All these engines had a cast iron block and a cast-iron cylinder head; by contrast, the Rover 60 car engines had an aluminium alloy cylinder head. Both block and head were spray-painted before machining, with the result that their machined surfaces are unpainted. On the earliest engines, the paint was a dark blue-green, but later engines (probably from some time in 1949) had a blue-grey finish. "Engine Blue", as it is known,

the Solihull operation was transferred to the newly opened Rover plant at Pengam near Cardiff.

Reconditioned engines were delivered to Rover agents, who were then required to stamp the number of the vehicle's original engine (as shown in the logbook or other vehicle documentation) into the cylinder block of the reconditioned unit. In many cases, this was not done, and in some cases the chassis number was used instead.

ENGINE NUMBERS 1948-1953

Identifying numbers for all engines are stamped at the top front of the cylinder block on the left-hand side, next to the water pump.

Note that these tables separate prefix from serial number with a dash to aid clarity. This dash is not found on the engines themselves.

Commencing numbers only are shown.

1948 and 1949 models	86-0001
1950 models	0610-0001
	(with L prefix on LHD models)
	0710-0001 (2-litre prototypes)
1951 models	1610-0001 (RHD)
	1613-0001 (LHD)
1952 models	2610-0001 (RHD)
	2613-0001 (LHD)
1953 models	3610-0001 (RHD)
	3613-0001 (LHD)

FACTORY RECONDITIONED NUMBERS

Part numbers

245579 1948-1950 engine, originally numbered up to 0610-0200
245581 1950-1951 engine, originally numbered from 0610-0201
245583 1952-1953 engine

Differences from standard

A typical number might be S0015/20/10, which can be interpreted as below. Alternatives for each position in the string are shown inset.

S   Engine reconditioned at Solihull
    K = reconditioned at Pengam (Cardiff)
    L = reconditioned at the London service depot in Seagrave Road
0015 Serial number, in this case the 15th of its type
20   Increase in bore size in thousandths of an inch (ie +20 bore)
    90 = liners fitted with standard bore
    91 = liners fitted with 0.10in bore increase
    92 = liners fitted with 0.20in bore increase
10   Under-size of a re-ground crankshaft in thousandths of an inch

ENGINE, TRANSMISSION & EXHAUST

Looking like new, this is the engine bay of a carefully restored August 1949 model with the 1.6-litre engine.

can be bought today from specialist Paint Man (www.paint-man.co.uk)

All engines had a pressed steel cover on the exhaust side of the engine to give access to the valve rockers, and this was painted black and secured by three brass nuts. However, only the earliest Land Rover engines had two detachable side-plates on the inlet side of the cylinder block, allowing access for maintenance. These side-plates were painted black and were made of steel, although those on the car engines were made of aluminium. The cylinder block was redesigned during 1949, with core plugs instead of the side-plates. This entered production (for the Land Rover only) in autumn 1949, but the changeover to the new type was not a clean one: Land Rovers continued to have the "side-plate" engine after the "core-plug" type had arrived, until supplies of the earlier blocks were exhausted.

The engine number is stamped into the top front of the cylinder block on the left-hand side. This is a 1948 engine, number R86-1383.

The two plates on the top of the rocker cover were probably originally the same red colour, but most have faded over the years. On later engines, they were attached with drive screws.

The oil filter canister on this 1948 engine displays its original AC manufacturer's decal.

The sump was fabricated from steel and was always finished in black; car engines and the pre-production Land Rovers had an aluminium sump. On most 1.6-litre engines, this sump had a distinct "step" in its profile (originally designed to clear the P3 saloon's steering gear), but very late examples had the redesigned sump used on the 2-litre engines, which had a more gently curved profile. With the redesigned sump came a new oil pump. The change was made at engine numbers 1610-2272 and 1613-1649 in 1951. Rover literature referred to the curved sump as the "shallow strengthened" type, and a kit of parts was made available to convert engines with the early stepped sump to the later type.

Much earlier, a change had been made to the oil sump filter, which had a reduced number of threads from engine number 86-0645, down from five to three. The change was intended to prevent incorrect setting of the filter, and Rover dealers were encouraged to modify earlier engines, stamping a letter O on the head of the filter plug to indicate that the change had been made. A few months after this came improved dust sealing for the sump, from engine number 86-5549.

Carburettor (1.6-litre)

All these engines had a single Solex 32 PBI2 carburettor mounted on a water-heated inlet manifold. Rover provided the following details of the choke and jet sizes:

Choke size	23
Main jet	139cc (102.5); a 107.5 size was used later
Air correction jet	160
Slow-running jet	45
Pump or speed jet	50
Economy jet	50

Early carburettors had a die-cast zinc-base throttle abutment plate, which could contract and leave the nuts loose, so from January 1949 there was a steel replacement, which came with tab washers for the nuts. This was a mandatory service modification, so it is unlikely that any carburettors still survive with the original die-cast plate.

By January 1949, the carburettor had also gained a new accelerator pump linkage so that the pump would operate only during the first stages of throttle opening and not over most of the throttle range. Dealers were recommended to convert older carburettors to the new specification if customers complained of a weak mixture flat spot during acceleration.

There was also a change to the elbow on top of the carburettor, which was rounded on early vehicles but from 0610-0280 took on a more oval shape. This change was apparently made to prevent the bonnet fouling the elbow when the spare wheel was mounted on it. This change to the elbow took place in August 1949 at the same time as dust-proofing improvements to the air cleaner (see below).

Very early inlet manifolds, possibly only on the first 150 or so production engines, also had a brass drain tube that ran down the side of the cylinder block and vented to atmosphere; this was the same as the system used on the car engines. On later Land Rover engines, the drain hole was blanked off.

Fuel system (1.6-litre)

Fuel was supplied to the carburettor by an SU type AUA 58L electric pump mounted to a bracket on the right-hand side of the bulkhead in the engine compartment (left-hand side when standing looking at the engine). The body of the pump had a dull black chemical finish, but its rear mounting flange was unpainted. The bracket on the bulkhead was initially in black-painted steel, and later in unpainted alloy.

The fuel pump drew petrol through an AC sediment filter with a glass bowl, mounted on a bracket lower down on the bulkhead. On early engines, the sediment filter had a long threaded pipe at the top and a round knob on the tap. This continued in use alongside one with a short threaded pipe at the top and a rectangular metal tap grip with turned-up edges, but it is not clear when this second type was introduced. The body of the sediment filter was always unpainted, but the bracket holding it to the bulkhead had a black chemical finish.

The 10-gallon (45-litre) fuel tank was mounted below the seat box on the right-hand side of the chassis frame, bolted to its own outrigger and to the one directly ahead of it. Most tanks had a protective undershield, but very early examples did not. The tank was filled through a screw-off cap in the top. This cap had a knurled rim. Early caps were painted a semi-gloss black but later ones were nickel-plated.

The earliest tanks were plated with Manchester plate, a form of tinplate, and their undershields were painted in the body colour. As the plating proved unsuccessful, later tanks were painted silver to match the chassis, and the undershield was painted to match. When the chassis colour changed to green, the tank and undershield were both painted black, and tanks thereafter remained black irrespective of the chassis colour.

Near to the filler cap on the top of the tank was an electric sender unit for the fuel gauge. This sender unit was always held in place by six half-inch 3BA screws.

Air cleaner (1.6-litre)

The air cleaner was always an AC oil-bath type, mounted behind the battery. The black canister with centrifugal pre-cleaner always looked the same, and on most 1.6-litre models was held to its base plate by toggle clamps. The fixings were simplified some time around June or July 1949.

Towards the middle of 1951, at chassis number 1610-0603, different mounting arrangements were introduced, with a metal strap running over the top of the air cleaner (see also the chassis chapter). A black rubber pipe was also added between the air cleaner elbow and the rocker cover.

There were some additional running changes to the air cleaner and its ancillaries over the years. From chassis number 866-6574 in June 1949, a restrictor was added to the elbow to help keep dust out of the engine. Then at chassis 0610-0165 a connecting tube assembly was added, and from 0610-0280 in August 1949 the dust sealing of the whole assembly and its connections was improved; dealers were recommended to carry out the modifications on existing vehicles as well. At the same time, the air cleaner elbow lost its sliding clamp and was secured to the air cleaner body by two wing nuts. Finally, at chassis number 0610-3414, a further rubber connection was added between the pipe and the rocker cover.

Details (1.6-litre)

Most of the other visible elements of the engine had a bare-metal finish. These included the front cover of the engine (made from light alloy), the inlet manifold and the water pipe leading to it from the front of the engine. Both the oil filler pipe at the front of the engine and its cap were cast from aluminium alloy and were unpainted. The oil filler cap was a screw-on type and was secured to the filler tube by a spring clip on the end of a short chain.

Early inlet manifolds, used until some time in the 1949 season, were the Rover P3 car type with two tapped holes; on the car, these were used for mounting the oil filter, but they were redundant on the Land Rover engine. Dust-sealing of the inlet manifold was improved from engine number 86-2599. The exhaust manifold originally had an unpainted cast iron finish that can be recreated quite successfully with modern heat-resistant paints.

1.6-LITRE ENGINE DETAILS

A few other points of detail might be helpful to anyone restoring one of these engines.

Dipstick
There were three different types. The first type had no locking spring and was used up to and including engine number 86-5713; the second type had a locking spring to improve dust sealing; and the third, associated with the curved sump, had a longer tube guide.

Exhaust valve seat inserts
These were always made of Brimochrome.

Exhaust valve oil seals
These were initially in the valve spring cap, but at engine number 061-06720, they were moved to the tops of the inlet valve guides to give better sealing.

Flywheel
Flywheels normally had a timing mark, stamped FA 15°, which indicates the firing point of no 1 cylinder, although some early flywheels had only a single TDC/FA line. They also had an EP marking to indicate the point at which no1 exhaust valve should be fully open.

Ignition timing
This was retarded from 15 degrees BTDC to 10 degrees BTDC to cure misfires, in September 1950.

Pistons
The original ones were supplied by either Specialloid or Lo-Ex, the two types being very similar in appearance. During 1950, a change was made to slotted-skirt types, at engine numbers 1610-2462 and 1613-1765.

The "side plate" engines gave way to the "core plug" type, which is illustrated here. Once again, this is a carefully restored example, in this case a 2-litre.

The top rocker cover was another unpainted item cast from aluminium alloy (it was not polished, either), and carried a pair of red plates, the left-hand one in printed alloy and giving details of the tappet clearances, while the right-hand one was painted brass and had details of patents used on the vehicle. The rocker cover on early engines was the P3 car type, in which there was a recess for the fixing nuts, but most engines had the later type with a flat collar beneath the nuts; this was a stronger design that was presumably more resistant to over-tightening. The securing nuts themselves were always made of nickel-plated brass.

There were variations in the thermostat housing, another unpainted item. On 1948 and early 1949 engines, it had two BSP-threaded plugs that were absent from later examples. However, the early type of housing continued to be fitted when a heater was ordered, because the heater connections tapped into it. Thermostat housings on engines up to 0611-2000 in mid-1950 also had bolts with special threaded heads to accept the bracket for the optional engine governor. These same engines had a double fan pulley to take the drive belt for the governor; on engines from August 1950 the double pulley was an option only fitted with the governor.

Two types of water pump were used. The early type, with part number 233161, looks very similar to the later type (part number 241884), but on the later pump the thermostat drilling at the top is counterbored to take a sealing ring and threaded to take an adaptor.

THE 2-LITRE ENGINE

The prototype 2-litre engines

The 2-litre engines of the experimental batch built in 1950 were visually similar to the 1.6-litre engine of the time and quite different in many respects from the later production 2-litre engines. These engines had the later production dimensions with the bore size increased from 2¾in (69.5mm) to 3in (77.8mm). They had no by-pass oil filter; the exhaust valves were shortened by 1/5in, and the carburettor had larger jets and a larger choke. There was also an access plate for the water gallery bolted to the top rear of the cylinder block.

These engines were all numbered with an 0710- prefix. A total of 50 were used in the trial batch of prototype vehicles, but a larger number would certainly have been made, if only to provide a service float. Engine number 0710-0051 was put into the prototype Fire Engine (on pre-production model R.06, originally built with a 1.6-litre engine), perhaps to ensure that the proposed production model would be adequately powered.

Production 2-litre

Rover literature was not consistent in its claims for the 2-litre engine, quoting the compression ratio as both 6.7:1 and 6.8:1, and the power output as both 58bhp and 52bhp. Nevertheless, the important torque figure was consistently shown as 101 lb ft at 1500rpm, and the swept volume as 1997cc. Bore and stroke were unchanged from the 1950 prototype batch.

Early 2-litre engines left the factory with their ignition timing set to suit the low-grade petrol that was still common in many export territories. The quality of petrol gradually improved in the early 1950s, and Rover felt able to advance the ignition timing a little as a result. So from April 1953, the ignition timing was set at 10 degrees BTDC on the assembly lines and the FA mark on the flywheel was altered to suit. Service literature stated that this timing was suitable for petrol with an octane rating of 80 or higher – which is a very clear indication of how low the octane rating of petrol must have been in the period when the 80-inch models were first available!

External features (2-litre)

The cylinder block and cylinder head were painted the same blue-grey colour as the later 1.6-litre engines, and all engines had the curved sump introduced on the late 1.6-litre types. The water gallery access plate at the top rear of the cylinder block was carried over from the prototype engines.

There were some visual differences from the 1.6-litre engines. Most obvious was that the top rocker cover had a breather at the front, and as a result these engines did not have the closed-circuit fume-recycling system used on the 1.6-litre types. The breather was finished in black and carried a label with white lettering that read "AC Air Cleaner. Wash thoroughly in petrol every 5000 miles. Re-oil gauze with engine oil." The first 200 engines had the same type of oil filler and cap as the 1.6-litre engines, but from engine number 2610-0201 the arrangements were changed. The filler tube was made integral with the pressed side rocker cover and was finished in the same black, and instead of a screw cap it had a push-on breather cap similar to the one for the rocker cover breather.

By July 1952, a problem had been identified with the bolts between the engine mountings and the cylinder block working loose. So a plate with locking tabs for the two bolts on each mounting was fitted on production, and the same plate could be fitted to earlier vehicles in place of the spring washers that had been standard.

Carburettor and fuel system (2-litre)

The carburettor on the 2-litre engines was the same Solex 32 PBI2 as on the earlier engines, but with different jets and choke. The air cleaner was essentially the same as on the late 1.6-litre engines, and was held in place by a metal strap that ran over the top of it. However, there was no tube running between the air cleaner elbow and the crankcase breather on the engine.

The fuel pump, fuel tank, and the rest of the fuel system were the same as on the 1.6-litre models, but there were minor

The later type of dipstick and the intricate securing arrangements for its tube are seen here on a 2-litre engine.

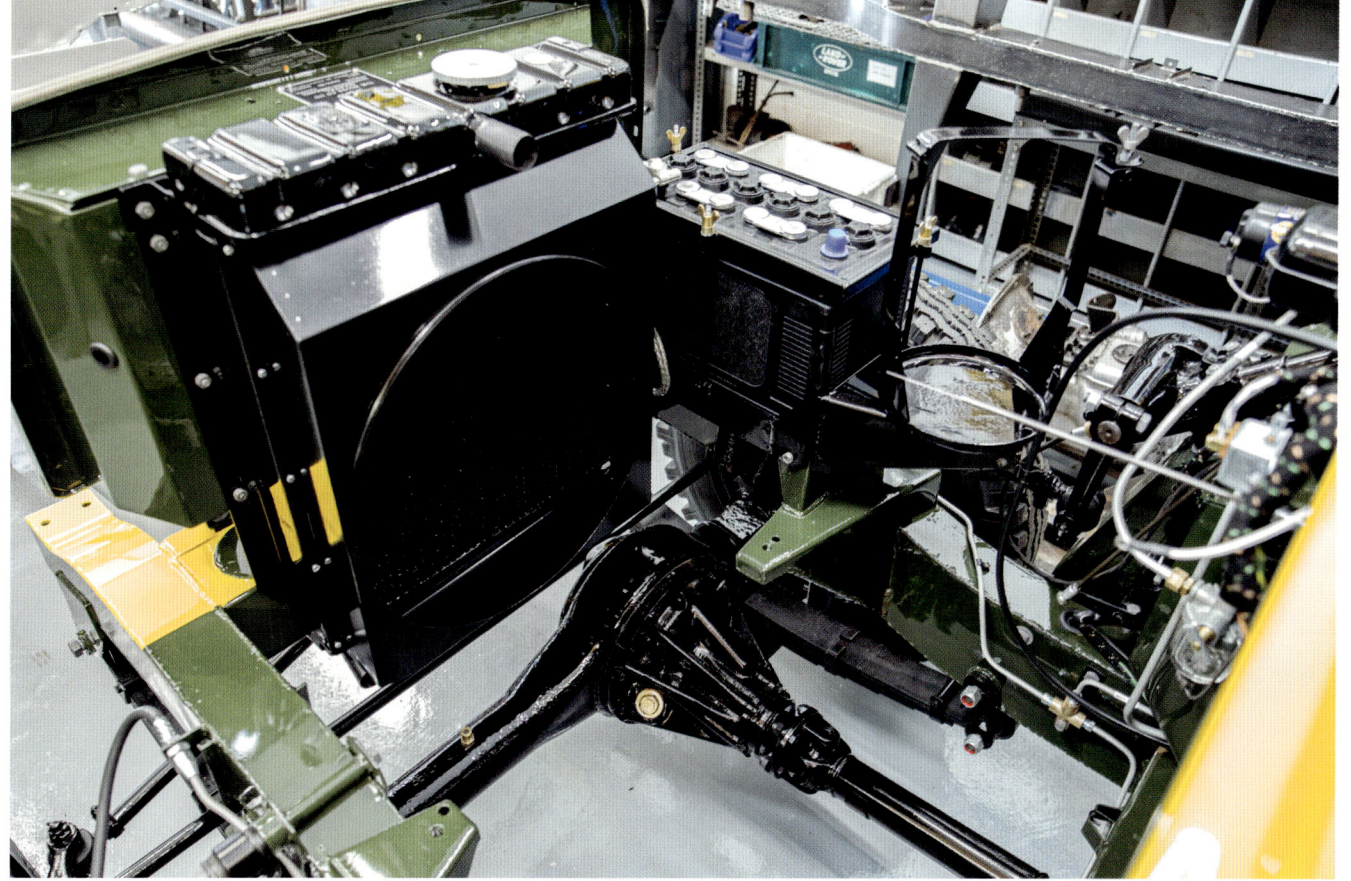

The engine bay without its engine: this is the 1953 AA vehicle (which explains the yellow paint). Clear here are the details of the radiator and fan cowl, and the bracket for the air cleaner.

differences associated with the sediment filter. Both types of sediment filter associated with the 1.6-litre engines were also used on the 2-litres, and there was a third type that was distinguished by a hooked tubular tap grip.

Cooling system (1.6-litre and 2-litre)

The cooling system is wholly conventional, with a water pump, radiator, fan, thermostat and rubber hoses.

The water pump was mounted at the front of the engine and was a centrifugal type driven from the crankshaft pulley by a rubber belt. The early water pump impellor had two ¾in (19mm) slots to locate the carbon ring, but the 1950-season engines had a new impellor and seal, which were recommended as a modification after November 1949.

The thermostat was mounted in an alloy housing at the front of the cylinder head above the water pump body, to which it was connected by a short tube and a rubber joint ring.

The radiator was mounted to the grille panel and had a cowl to improve the efficiency of the cooling fan on the nose of the water pump. Original radiators were made by Serck and had a small tag soldered to their header tanks, giving the maker's name and a batch number. From late 1948, the

Seen here correctly restored with its original Manchester plate finish, this is the fuel tank on 1948 model R86-0027. There was no undershield on these early tanks.

This early plated tank has the correct finish for the filler cap. The fuel pipe and gauge fittings are also correct.

On this August 1949 model, the fuel tank and its undershield were both painted black.

The seat cushion had to be removed to gain access to the fuel filler in the top of the tank. Note the sender unit and the small cutout in the seat base that gives clearance around it.

This is a 1953 petrol tank, with the correct black finish and unpainted filler cap. Note also the four-bolt fixing for the sender unit rather than the three-bolt type used earlier.

header tank also carried a soldered circular tag with the date of manufacture, which is expressed in numbers, eg 10/49. Early header tanks had recessed pressings, but later ones had ridges, and there was a slightly larger cowl on early models.

The earliest radiator cores had fin-and-tube construction, but by 1950 a slatted core was in use. The standard radiator pressure cap was a 4 psi type, and had a short chain running to a T-piece inside the neck. A 15 psi radiator cap was used in conjunction with the optional oil cooler (see Optional Equipment). The fan, radiator core and header tank were all painted black.

The water hoses – on the radiator, on the water pump, and on the pipe leading to the inlet manifold hot-spot – were originally fixed by wire-type spring clamps, and not by the more modern Jubilee clips.

Exhaust & mounting bracket (1.6 & 2-litre)

The exhaust manifold was on the left of the engine and the exhaust pipe always emerged horizontally to pass through the wing before sweeping down behind the left-hand front wheel and then under the chassis to emerge behind one of the rear wheels.

It consisted of two sections, which were a long front pipe running from the manifold, and a silencer box with tailpipe fitted transversely within the rear of the chassis frame. They were attached to one another through a conventional three-bolt flange. There were several different versions of this system, but replacements have always tended to be to the latest specification, and few restorers are very concerned about the precise details of the original system. For completeness, however, the details were as follows. There were two types of front pipe, and three types of rear exhaust system.

On 1948 and 1949 models up to and including chassis number 866-5603, the front pipe had no heat shields. It was supported in two places. The front mounting was a wire bracket attached to the bulkhead outrigger, supporting a cotton-reel type bush. A cranked rod inserted through this bush was in turn bolted through a welded bracket on the exhaust pipe. The rear support was a triangular bracket at the rear end of the pipe, containing an eye for another cotton-reel bush. A long bolt with a nut and two washers of different sizes then secured this to the chassis frame.

On later 1949 models, the front pipe changed to a different type, probably as the result of a report on two pre-production

When heat shields were added to the exhaust, they were initially bolted in place.

The later exhaust heat shields were welded to the pipe, as here.

The exhaust pipe passes through the inner wing. Visible in its large clip, also on the inner wing, is the bonnet prop rod with its rubber sleeve that helps to prevent rattles.

The rear exhaust silencer is seen here on a 1951 right-hand-drive model.

The exhaust support bracket that was welded to the early tailpipe tended to fracture.

The clamp-type rear exhaust support bracket was introduced early in the 1950 season.

Land Rovers that was published in August 1949 by the National Institute of Agricultural Engineering. This second type of front pipe had no support under the bulkhead outrigger, and was found on all subsequent 80-inch models, being used as a service replacement for the original type. It was distinguished by a pair of heat shields, which on very early examples were attached by clamps, nuts and bolts, but on later ones were welded in place.

The early type of rear exhaust was used up to late November 1950, and was arranged so that the tailpipe emerged below the rear cross-member of the right-hand side of the vehicle. This necessitated an angled "kink" in the pipe. Some countries that took left-hand-drive models, however, did not want the exhaust on the kerb side of the vehicle, so all left-hand-drive Land Rovers were given a redesigned tail section with inlet and exhaust pipes at the same end of the silencer box, so that the tailpipe emerged behind the left-hand rear wheel. This is usually known as the "handed" tailpipe.

All the non-handed tailpipes were supported by a single mounting, and on early examples there was a bracket welded to the pipe. From some time in 1949 a redesign led to the bracket becoming integral with the exhaust. On right-hand-drive models up to and including 0611-1063, the tailpipe support bracket passed over a threaded support rod on the chassis, a rubber cotton-reel bush was interposed between the two, and the assembly was held in place by a nut on the rod. The support rod itself passed right through the chassis rail and its other end was used as the mounting pin for the left-hand rear damper. The rod was absent from later right-hand-drive chassis, which instead had a bolt that passed through the cotton-reel bush and into the chassis.

The early type of welded bracket tended to fracture, and in approximately November 1949, at chassis number 0611-1383, Rover introduced a new type of mounting. This type was secured by a clamp and pinch-bolts. Pattern exhausts have always had a variety of different tailpipe brackets, usually to suit the capabilities or budgets of their manufacturers!

The "handed" tailpipes were fitted to left-hand-drive Land Rovers from 1613-1574, 1623-0081, 1633-0001 and 1663-0025. These tailpipes had a unique fixing system and were supported in two places, one being a bracket welded to the tailpipe and the other a saddle-type clamp on the pipe.

TRANSMISSION

The 1948, 1949 and 1950 model Land Rovers all had a permanent four-wheel-drive system with a freewheel in the front driveline to compensate for different rotational speeds between front and rear axles. This system was dropped in October 1950 for the 1951 models, and the new system gave selectable four-wheel drive in High range. Four-wheel drive was still permanently engaged in Low range. Some of the trial batch of 2-litre prototypes built in early 1950 also had the selectable system.

ENGINE, TRANSMISSION & EXHAUST

This is the full transmission in an early 1948 production model, number R86-0038. The primary gearbox is furthest from the camera, the transfer box is nearer the camera with the transmission brake on its rear output, and bolted to the front of the transfer box is the freewheel casing. This is the early type of casing with a cast boss on each side.
(Peter Galilee)

This time pictured from the other side, this is the full transmission assembly on a 1953 2-litre model.

Bellhousing

All models of 80-inch Land Rover had essentially the same bellhousing. However, dust ingress gave problems on more than one occasion. A running change was made in approximately January 1950 when a dust seal was added to the aperture in the top of the bell housing. This was carried out at gearbox number 0610-2416 (RHD), but rather later on LHD models, at gearbox number L0610-4469. There were then further changes to the dust sealing arrangements from gearbox numbers 2610-0201 (right-hand drive) and 2613-1503 (left-hand drive) in late 1952. The additional rubber seals and grommets introduced at this stage could be fitted retrospectively to earlier gearboxes if required.

Clutch

The single-dry-plate clutch always had a 9-inch diameter. The very earliest models had a Rover clutch but a Borg & Beck type soon followed, and became the only type stocked by the Spares Department.

The so-called Rover clutch was actually manufactured by Newton, and was used with engines up to and including number 0610-0200 in approximately August 1949. It always came with a Borg & Beck clutch plate. The early Borg & Beck

The clutch and ring gear are seen here on a restored 2-litre engine.

Primary gearbox

The four-speed main gearbox was essentially the same as that in Rover cars of the time, with synchromesh on third and top gears only. The P3 type of gearbox was fitted until approximately the end of 1949, and after that the P4 saloon type was used, with its higher third gear ratio. The later gearboxes were numbered from 0610-6001.

The exact gear ratios were as follows:

	Early gearbox	From 0610-6001
First	2.996:1	2.996:1
Second	2.043:1	2.043:1
Third	1.490:1	1.377:1
Top	1.000:1	1.000:1
Reverse	2.547:1	2.547:1

Transfer gearbox

The two-speed transfer gearbox had gear ratios of 1.148:1 in High range and 2.888:1 in Low range. Production examples had a pressed steel bottom cover plate, but the pre-production transfer boxes had a cast aluminium bottom cover. Early casings were sand-cast, but the later ones were die-cast. Transfer boxes fitted with a freewheel had an additional cast housing for this between the main casing and the front output shaft housing.

The early transfer boxes had an oil capacity of six pints, but this was found in service to be too much and to cause leaks. So the capacity was reduced to four pints during 1950, and a service modification was introduced to bring earlier transfer boxes up to the new standard. This involved tapping a new level plug into the side of the casting about 7/8in below the original plug, and transfer boxes that now have two level plugs were obviously subject to this modification. Late transfer boxes also had a much smaller oil level plug than early ones, and some (probably those made at around the change-over point) had the small plug with an adapter to suit the earlier larger drilling.

There were other minor changes to the casing in the early days. On the very first transmissions, there was insufficient clearance to use a spanner or socket on one of the bolts securing the transfer box to the main gearbox. At first, a small relief was chiselled into the transfer box casing to improve access, and subsequently a channel was cast into the top of this casing to resolve the problem permanently. The method of attaching the speedometer drive cable to the transfer box output also changed; on early models, there was a brass retaining piece, but from 0610-5831 in late December 1949 this changed to a retaining washer and three bolts.

A further external difference between early and late transfer boxes does not appear to have coincided with any internal changes. Up to and including gearbox 86-2380, the transfer lever cover plate on the top right of the casing was secured by set screws. On later transfer boxes, the plate was retained by

clutches had coarse splines on the cross-shaft of the withdrawal mechanism.

The later clutches were completely manufactured by Borg & Beck. They were introduced on the new Rover P4 saloons in autumn 1949 and were introduced on Land Rovers at the same time. These later clutches had fine splines on the cross-shaft of the withdrawal mechanism, and were accompanied by a different engine flywheel.

set bolts with washers.

The changeover to the transfer box that allowed two-wheel drive (to the rear wheels) in High range occurred early in the 1951 season, in late November 1950. The chassis numbers at which the change was made were 1610-0603, 1613-1573 and 1616-0909, 1663-0025 and 1666-0787. Service literature also quoted the change as taking place at gearbox numbers 1610-2314 for right-hand-drive models and 1613-1688 for left-hand-drive types.

The "selectable" transfer boxes contained a dog clutch, operated by an additional control lever, that disconnected drive to the front axle. They also had an increased oil capacity of 4.5 pints (2.5 litres), and their casings had a different housing for the speedometer drive. This was further modified from gearbox numbers 2610-1454 and 2613-0447 by the addition of a mudshield to the rear face of the housing.

Freewheel

The freewheel allowed the rear wheels to "over-run" the front pair, absorbing slip between front and rear wheels and preventing damaging axle wind-up with the permanent four-wheel drive system.

The freewheel itself was similar in principle to the one fitted to Rover cars, but in practice shared only a small number of components with the car type. It was operated by a cable (from a ring-pull control in the floor) until late 1949, and from gearbox number 0610-4015 it was rod-operated. Early castings for the freewheel housing had a boss on either side, and later housings had a boss on only one side with a clearly visible "scar" on the other side where the die had been altered. However, this change appears not to have coincided with any internal changes.

Some pre-production Land Rovers had both a freewheel and a selectable four-wheel drive system, and it was some time before all traces of this arrangement disappeared from production models. Very early production gearboxes (up to and including gearbox number 86-1988) incorporated a locking dog for this selectable system, although it was permanently locked by a steel spacer ring in the selector mechanism and could not be unlocked. The freewheel fitted to later gearboxes has a simpler design without the locking dog.

Propshafts

The front and rear propshafts were Hardy Spicer types with a sliding joint in each to absorb axle movement. They were always finished in black. There were shafts of different lengths to suit the earlier long-nose and later short-nose differentials.

Very early propshafts for use with the long-nose differential were made of thinner-gage metal than later types, although the two were interchangeable and later types were certainly fitted to early models as service replacements. There were also two different types of propshaft for use with the later short-nose differentials. The difference between them lay in the fixings between the yokes and the drive flanges on the transfer box output shaft and the differential. The earlier type suited the P3 type differentials with their circular drive flanges, and the later type suited the P4 type differentials with their square drive flanges. The change took place at gearbox number 0610-6001 and (theoretically) at axle number 0610-6001 as well.

GEARBOX NUMBERS 1948-1953

Identifying numbers for all main gearboxes were stamped on the right-hand side of the gearbox casing, at the rear.

Identifying numbers for all transfer gearboxes were stamped on the top of the casing.

Note that these tables separate prefix from serial number with a dash to aid clarity. This dash is not found on the units themselves.

Commencing numbers only are shown.

1948 and 1949 models
86-0001 (with L prefix on LHD models)

1950 models
0610-0001 (with L prefix on LHD models)

1951 models
1610-0001 (RHD)
1613-0001 (LHD)

1952 models
2610-0001 (RHD)
2613-0001 (LHD)

1953 models
3610-0001 (RHD)
3613-0001 (LHD)

Rover operated a reconditioning scheme for gearboxes that was similar to the one for engines. A factory reconditioned gearbox would be fitted with an identifying brass plate. The full details of the codes that reveal the specification differences from standard are not available, but it does appear that gearboxes used the same prefix codes as engines to indicate where the reconditioning was done. These were K (Pengam, after 1964 approximately), L (London, Seagrave Road Service Depot) and S (Solihull factory).

BODYWORK (LOWER)

For ease of reference, this book divides the Land Rover's body into two areas – the lower bodywork and the canvas or metal superstructure. This chapter covers the bulkhead, seatbox and cab floor, back body or tub, tailboard, doors, wings, front panel, grille, bonnet, windscreen and frame. It also has separate sections for paint colours and badges.

The next chapter looks at the superstructure – sidescreens, canvas hoods, hoodsticks, hardtop and truck cab.

Body – construction

The Land Rover body used aluminium alloy panels with some steel stiffening members to add rigidity. The front bulkhead was (normally) made of steel, and the back body was reinforced by galvanised steel cappings.

The aluminium alloy used for the body panels of production 80-inch models was Birmabright BB2; pre-production models had Duralumin panels. Birmabright was the trade name of various type of lightweight alloy metal sheet manufactured by Birmetals Ltd, of Clapgate Lane, Quinton in Birmingham. These alloys were introduced by the Birmid Group in 1929 and an early use was for the bodywork of George Eyston's Land Speed Record Car, Thunderbolt. The high corrosion resistance of Birmabright led to its use in various wartime applications.

The BB2 variant consisted of 2% magnesium, 0.25% manganese, and 97.5% aluminium. Birmetals no longer exists and the Birmabright designations are obsolete, but modern equivalent designations are British Standard NS4, American Standard 5251, and ISO designation AlMg2.

Bulkhead

The steel bulkhead was quite literally central to the construction of the Land Rover body, which was built up around it and depended on it for correct alignment of its components. All bulkheads were bolted to the front outriggers on the chassis, just ahead of the gearbox cross-member. (Note that Rover service literature did not call this component a bulkhead, but preferred to describe it as a dash panel.)

As a steel component, the bulkhead can rust badly, and in particular around the mounting area for the steering box. This is constructed from layers of sheet steel, and water can get between the sheets and seriously weaken the steering box mounting platform. Several specialists over the years have manufactured pattern bulkhead replacements, many of which are indistinguishable from the originals. The only caveat when buying one of these is to order the right type, as the bulkhead did vary over nearly five years of 80-inch production. There were three standard types, plus one special type.

On the first 1500 production Land Rovers (that is, to chassis number 86-1500 in December 1948), the bulkhead was fabricated from folded steel. It had a detachable centre panel that incorporated the front section of the transmission tunnel, and the cut-out that fitted around the bell-housing had straight edges. On the front face, near the top on each side, was a welded housing for the sidelight. An elongated oval mounting box for the instrument panel was welded to its inner face in the centre at the top and the whole assembly was painted in the body colour. A quirk of interest to restorers is that these bulkheads were made with an apparently unnecessary hole on each side for a captive nut; in practice, it was used during assembly to take a 3/16in bolt that located the steering box while it was being bolted in place.

Two galvanised catches for the windscreen fasteners were bolted to the inner face of the bulkhead, and the vehicles built after autumn 1948 had a galvanised handrail bolted across the upper section. (The handrail was an extra-cost option before November 1948.) Sealing between the bottom of the windscreen and the top of the bulkhead was effected by a rubber seal attached to the underside of the windscreen frame. The windscreen pivot plates (often known as "eagle's heads" after their later shape) on these early bulkheads also had a flat top.

The second type of bulkhead was introduced in December 1948 at chassis 86-1501 and was pressed from steel; by this stage, Rover had clearly realised that the Land Rover would be a strong seller and was now prepared to invest in some press-tools for the body. These bulkheads did not have a detachable centre panel, and they had a curved cut-out to clear the bell-housing. They had the same sidelight housings and instrument mounting box as the earlier type, the same galvanised windscreen catches, and the same galvanised handrail. This time, the sealing rubber was attached to the top of the bulkhead

On the first 1500 production models, the bulkhead had a detachable centre panel, with the angular appearance seen here. Note also on this autumn 1948 model the blanking plate for the steering column cut-out on the passenger side, and the rectangular access cover on the gearbox tunnel.

Both the shape of the "eagle's heads" and the windscreen pivot bolts that passed through them went through some evolutions. These are on an August 1949 model.

rather than to the bottom of the windscreen frame.

The optional heater was introduced during the currency of this second type of bulkhead, and when one was fitted its fixing holes had to be drilled by hand first. From May 1949, the six fixing holes were pre-drilled in the bulkhead so that less work was required to fit the heater. This change took place at chassis number 866-5608. The "eagle's heads" on these bulkheads had a curved top, and it is easy to see from their shape how the distinctive nickname came about.

The third type of bulkhead was introduced in summer 1951. It was essentially the same as the second type but no longer had mountings for the sidelights on its upper front face. There were some more minor differences, the lower housings for the door hinges being shorter than on earlier bulkheads while the holes for some of the controls were in different positions. This final type of production bulkhead was introduced at chassis numbers 1610-3899, 1613-6866, 1616-3018, 1623-0081, 1626-0081, 1630-0005, 1633-0008, 1636-0010, 1663-0079 and 1666-2023. The "eagle's heads" also changed again to a flat-topped type.

The first two types of bulkhead could develop cracks around the area of the steering box mounting. So in late 1952 a Service modification was introduced, which involved fitting

The distinctive angular shape and bolted bonnet hinge receivers of the fabricated bulkhead are seen here on Land Rovers built some three years apart. The green one is an 0610-series model, and the other a 3610-series model.

a strengthening plate to the driver's side of the bulkhead and bolting the steering box through this. The plate could be welded or bolted to the bulkhead and was clearly visible just above the pedals.

All bulkheads had open flange-type mountings for the door hinges welded to their outer edges. As noted above, the lower hinge mountings changed in summer 1951. Bulkheads

Bulkheads were drilled so that they could be used on either LHD or RHD models, and redundant holes were blanked off on production. This is the blanking plate for the steering column on a RHD vehicle. Most were made of aluminium, but the rust here shows that this is an early steel example.

were also pre-drilled to suit either LHD or RHD and for an engine governor. Redundant holes were covered by riveted plates, which were steel on the first 200 or so vehicles and then changed to aluminium alloy.

A few vehicles were built with a fabricated bulkhead, made from angle iron with flat and straight-folded BB2 panels riveted in place. The legendary "aluminium bulkhead" also had a rigid steel foot, to which the steering box was bolted. No reference to this has been found in any Land Rover service literature, and the reason for the existence of these bulkheads remains controversial. The popular belief for many years was that the aluminium bulkheads were manufactured to keep production going when the press tool for the steel bulkhead failed, but this is highly unlikely to be true. Hand-making bulkheads to maintain supplies to the assembly line would have slowed production down very noticeably, and there are no indications that this happened.

Some painstaking research carried out by the Land Rover Series One Club was published in the December 2010 issue of its magazine, *Legend*. This concluded that the fabricated bulkheads were mostly fitted to UK-market vehicles over the winters of 1951-1952 and 1952-1953. Examples of these bulkheads have been found on a few earlier 80-inch models, but it is possible that these were supplied as service replacements

BODYWORK (LOWER)

This 1953 model has a fabricated bulkhead, and the picture shows the distinctive steel "foot" support ahead of the footwell.

or were swapped from other vehicles. Examples of unused fabricated bulkheads – likely to have been service spares – have also been reported.

The most plausible explanation seems to be that Rover maintained a small stock of fabricated bulkheads against the possibility of supply shortages, and that supplies faltered for some reason over the winters of 1951-1952 and 1952-1953, with the result that several of these bulkheads were used on the assembly lines.

Seatbox and cab floor

The layout and construction of this area were the same on all 80-inch models, although there were multiple variations of detail. Essentially, the seatbox assembly was bolted to the body tub at the rear and incorporated sill panels that extended forwards to meet the bulkhead. There was a gearbox cover plate in the centre and a floor section on either side of it. The panels were all spot-welded together.

The seatbox ran right across the vehicle and had three apertures, each with a hinged lid. The lid on the right gave access to the fuel tank, the one in the centre gave access to the Centre PTO controls (when fitted), and the one on the left gave access to a stowage area. The front face of the seatbox, known as the heelboard, incorporated an inspection cover for the gearbox on some models (see below), and two apertures for the handbrake. The handbrake was positioned to suit left-hand-drive or right-hand drive as appropriate, and there was a blanking plate over the redundant aperture. Some very early models had two screw holes drilled alongside the large holes into which the rubber mountings for the seat cushion fit. These were for a blanking disc to be fitted over redundant holes when no passenger seat was fitted, and were deleted when the passenger seat became standard in autumn 1948.

On all 80-inch models the two outer seatbox lids each had two hinges. These were riveted to the lid, and their other ends were bolted to the angle plate running along the back of the seatbox. Each lid had a sherardised hasp screwed and bolted to its forward edge, and these hasps fitted over turnbuckles held to the heelboard by screws and nuts. Some seatbox lids had rubber protectors riveted to their front outer corners, and these seem to have been an optional fitment or possibly a Service modification to prevent rattles.

The seatbox lid over the petrol tank could be held open by a webbing retaining strap that was fixed to the capping on the body tub by a self-tapping screw; a hook on the other end of the strap simply hooked over the edge of the lid when it was open. Stiffeners were added under the locker lid at an unknown point before 1950, and these were designed to double as a holder for the vehicle handbook.

Between the two outer seatbox lids, the third hinged cover plate was initially rectangular. It then became shield-shaped in early 1950 when other modifications in this area were introduced (for commencing chassis numbers, see the notes on the "third stage" below). Both types of cover plate had a piano-type hinge at the rear and a spring clip at the front that kept them closed.

The variations elsewhere in this area of the vehicle are most easily understood through a chronological format, and there were two main stages of development. The first stage was associated with the first 1500 vehicles, and lasted until December 1948. The second stage then lasted until the end of 80-inch production, though with minor variations along the way.

On the first 1500 vehicles, the floor sections were integral with the seatbox assembly. These floor panels did not extend as far as the bulkhead, and the gap in each footwell was bridged by a separate toeplate made from sheet steel that was bolted in place. These toeplates all had holes for the pedals to pass through, and the redundant holes on the passenger's side were covered with a blanking plate. There were no weather shields for the pedals and controls in this area. Parts Catalogues claim that there was a cover-plate in the driver's side floor for the pedal adjuster on vehicles up to chassis number 86-0180 in mid-September 1948; in practice, this appears not to have been fitted to all such early vehicles, and was also fitted to some later ones!

The gearbox cover on these first 1500 Land Rovers was very angular and the gearbox inspection cover in the centre of the heelboard was removable. The cover plate for the reverse stop on the right-hand side of the gearbox cover was attached by two drive screws. There was an interesting anomaly on the first 150 or so production vehicles, where the bellhousing cover had a strip welded to each of its side ends. These covers were almost certainly leftover pre-production types that were used up on production. The positions of the fixing holes had been moved, and the strip was welded over them and drilled with holes in the correct places; the old holes remained visible on the reverse face of the cover.

From chassis number 86-1501, there were several modifications to suit the new pressed-steel bulkhead, and Rover introduced other improvements at the same time. The bell-housing cover in this second stage was much wider than before with a more rounded shape, and extended much further to the left of the vehicle centre-line. The floor panels were now separate from the seatbox, and the gearbox inspection cover in the centre of the heelboard was hinged.

Simple rubber weather shields were fitted around the major driving controls, and all were initially attached by capped rivets. The handbrake lever had a flat rubber shield that was attached to the heelboard, and from the start of the 1951 season there was a similar shield across the aperture for the transfer box control lever in the right-hand floor panel. The shield for the gear lever aperture was initially retained by capped rivets, but from chassis number 0610-1033 it was replaced by a new type with a shaped lip that retained it without the need for rivets.

There was a minor change in summer 1949, when a larger cover plate for the gearbox reverse stop was fitted to the bell-housing cover at chassis numbers 0610-3885, 0620-0094 and 0630-0022. The very last 1.6-litre models also had a removable gearbox inspection cover (in the heelboard) with fixing prongs, and this change may have coincided with the change to the reverse stop cover plate.

Back body (tub)

The back body, or body tub, was essentially an open box with four sides. The rear-facing side contained a drop-down tailboard and the whole assembly was made up from two main body halves, consisting of the outer panels and wheelboxes, and a floor panel. The whole body was made from BB2 alloy in 18swg (1.219mm) thickness, and reinforcement was provided by galvanised steel body cappings attached to the aluminium panels with rivets. The whole assembly was bolted to the chassis through vertical plates on the cross-members (see the earlier section on the Chassis Frame). The whole of the tub, including the floor but of course not the galvanised cappings, was painted in the body colour.

Rover made a rubber floor covering for the tub, as an optional extra, although many users fitted their own to protect the floor from damage. There were always stiffeners welded to the underside of the floor, and the ends of these were angled from approximately chassis number 0610-2501 to give additional clearance for the wiring harness. As 1952-season production began, they were again shortened to clear new bracing on the chassis. Then in June 1952, three more aluminium stiffeners were added under the floor to guard against damage from overloading. These were added at chassis numbers 2610-5377, 2613-5479, 2616-3400, 2630-0014, 2633-0014, 2636-0006, 2663-1986 and 2665-1015.

The front panel (that is, the one directly behind the cab seats) is often called the transom panel. It was initially straight, but from chassis number 0611-0305 in April 1950 its upper section was kinked backwards. This allowed room for the thicker "shovel" type seats with hinged backrests that were introduced at the same time (see the section on Seats, later). The two tail panels, one on either side of the tailboard opening, were pre-drilled to accept the rear lights. The left-hand panel carried a Land Rover oval badge, and the right-hand one was normally used for the registration plate – which of course varied from country to country.

There were several changes in this area in mid-1949. This

BODYWORK (LOWER)

This view of an 0610-series Land Rover shows the general layout of the back body, with the spare wheel in its standard position in a well behind the transom panel. The hood sticks can be seen in their sockets, and the arrangement of the tailboard chain and its securing hook can be seen.

The earliest models had staples on the sides of the tub to accept leather strap fixings attached to the hood.

From May 1949, cleats replaced the staples as hood fixings on the body sides.

was when the hood fixings changed from leather straps to rope (the so-called "bootlace" fixing; see below), and each tail panel acquired an extra Y-shaped lashing attachment to accept the rope, just below the corner capping. Each of these hooks was secured by a single screw that passed through the body panel to a nut on the inside face. Each tail panel was always braced to the adjacent wheelbox by a curved gusset panel, and at about the same time these gussets became noticeably narrower. These changes probably occurred at chassis 866-6001 in May, and shortly afterwards (at 866-6225 later the same month), the wheelboxes were pre-drilled on all models with the four holes needed for the optional rear seats which were then available only on export models.

All the exposed upper edges of the body were always protected and reinforced by galvanised steel cappings. The front capping carried various fittings for the cab seats (see the section on Seats later) and was narrower on the "kinked" front panel. Early front cappings had a separate door stop bolted to them, but from 0611-4761 in July 1950 different cappings were fitted with the door stops built into them. All four galvanised corner cappings incorporated sockets for the hoodsticks (see the section on Superstructure, below).

There were extra cappings on the top inboard edges of the tail panels, on either side of the tailboard opening. These incorporated dowels that were part of the tailboard securing system, and attached to them was a locking wedge that passed through a hole in the dowel to secure the eye fitting on the tailboard. In addition, there was a protective galvanised strip

61

across the tailboard opening at the rear of the floor (see the section on the Tailboard, below).

The spare wheel was normally stowed upright against the front panel of the body tub, where it was held by a special clamp with a spring clip. Clamp and spring clip changed at the same time as the kinked front panel was introduced, the later clamp being smaller than the original. The spare wheel could of course also be carried on the bonnet; for details of this mounting, see the Optional Equipment section.

There were also stowage clips inside the body tub for the starting handle and the jack handle. Each tool was secured by two sprung clips, the starting handle on the front panel and the jack extension bar on the left-hand side panel. For details of these tools, see the section on Tools. The inside of the front panel on early models also had two staples to which the straps of the three-seater hood (see below) attached. These were no longer fitted after 1950, when the three-seater hood was discontinued.

On the outside of each side panel were fittings to which the full hood could be secured. On early models, these fittings were staples, screwed through the panel with nuts on the inside. There were two on each panel. After the first 150 or so vehicles, thicker staples were used, presumably because the early ones had been prone to distortion. From chassis 866-6001 in May 1949, the staples were replaced by two cleats welded to each side, to suit the new method of hood fixing. These cleats were more closely spaced than the staples had been.

Tailboard

The tailboard remained essentially unchanged throughout 80-inch production, although it differed from tailboards on pre-production models. These had three external vertical braces instead of the one that was used on production models. The single rib on production models initially had a simple L-section but was later changed to a stronger top-hat section. This probably occurred in May 1949, at the same time as three cleats were welded near the top of the tailboard to accept the new rope fixing for the rear curtain.

Like the rest of the body, the tailboard was made from BB2 alloy with galvanised steel reinforcing cappings. One capping ran across the top edge and there was a capping down each side as well. These side cappings incorporated eyes that fitted over the dowels on the tail panels when the tailgate was closed. Between mid-1949 (theoretically from chassis 86-6001) and late 1949 (chassis numbers 0610-5462 and 0630-0027), the eyes incorporated rope cleats to suit the lacing of the "zig-zag" hood then in use (see the section on Canvas, below).

Tailboards had two large galvanised hinges that were bolted to their outer ends. Early hinges were slightly larger than the later ones that were introduced at chassis number 86-6001 in mid-1949. Bolted to the inside surface of the tailboard at each side was a plate with a hook for the support chain. Both support chains were galvanised and were initially sleeved in the khaki canvas used for the hoods; later ones had sleeves in Vynide of the same colour as the seats. The inboard end of each chain was attached to a hook bolted to the wheelbox on its own side.

There were no weather seals on the tailboard of the first 1500 Land Rovers. From chassis number 86-1501, rubber strips were then added at the bottom and sides, mainly to improve dust-sealing. The bottom strip was secured by a retaining strip held to the tailboard by rivets and pop rivets. The two side seals and their retaining plates were each in two sections, the upper one shorter than the lower one, and were retained in the same way. When Rover made another attempt at dust-proofing the Land Rover in September 1949, improved weather strips were added. This occurred at chassis number 0610-1747 on the assembly lines, but it was also possible to fit the new seals to older vehicles retrospectively.

Land Rovers exported to the USA had to have the rear number-plate mounted centrally on the tailboard to meet US traffic regulations. So a special bracket was fitted to the central support rib, accompanied by special lighting arrangements (see below). This bracket appears to have been hinged so that it would hang below the tailboard and display the number-plate to the rear if the vehicle was driven with the tailboard open.

RIVETS

Rover minimised the amount of welding needed in the bodywork of the Land Rover, preferring to use bolts and nuts or rivets wherever possible.

Rivets are a well-documented characteristic of the 80-inch models, and are most visible on the body cappings, where they hold these to the alloy panels. Rover used domed rivets with a tubular shaft, made of aluminium so that they were soft enough to fix by hand without the need for heating (which is necessary with steel rivets).

Old rivets can be removed in one of two ways. One way is to chisel off the head, but this should only be done when the head is against steel. Attempting to chisel a rivet head against aluminium alloy will damage the alloy before it removes the head. The other way is to centre-punch the domed head and then drill the rivet out. Note that the drilling should always be done from the manufactured domed head and not from the spread end of the rivet, which may not be central to the shaft. It is important to keep the drill straight and central in order not to damage any of the surrounding metal with it. A 3/16in drill bit is the best to use.

There is a technique to fitting new rivets. First, the metal sections to be joined should be clamped together to ensure a tight fit. The rivet is then fitted with the domed head on the inside of the panel. It is most easily set by squeezing between the jaws of rivet snaps. When using this special hand tool, the domed head of the rivet goes into a shaped recess (the anvil) and the other end is squeezed and flattened out against the metal by a domed setting head when the jaws are closed together. Rivets can also be set using a hammer, but a special anvil setting tool is then required as well.

Rivet sizes are quoted in shaft diameter and length. Note that if the rivet is the wrong length for the job in hand it will not form properly under squeezing, and if it is not set properly it may leave a gap between the two pieces being joined. It is always advisable to practice setting rivets in some scrap metal before tackling the real job, whichever method of setting is to be used.

The central rib on the tailboard was a simple L-section on early models such as the 1948 example illustrated, but by mid-1949 had changed to a stronger top-hat section. The three rope cleats were also a mid-1949 addition, to suit the latest hood securing arrangements.

This unusual view of a closed tailboard, seen from inside the vehicle, shows one of the two brackets holding the tailboard support chains.

The tailboard of a 1950 model is seen in the open position. The gloss paint finish of the inner surface did not survive long in use! Note the securing pegs with their safety chains, and the canvas covers for the tailboard chains. This vehicle has been fitted with non-standard amber turn indicator lights below its D-lamps.

Although similar in concept, the US-pattern central mounting bracket was not the same as that used on the Tickford Station Wagons.

Doors

The two side doors are perhaps more accurately described as half-doors, as they reach only up to waist height. Detachable sidescreens were available to create an upper half for each door and are described separately, below. The doors were an extra-cost option for the first few months of production, but were made standard from October 1948.

The doors never had a frame of their own but their alloy skins were folded back to create top and side sections that were reinforced with alloy stiffener plates. Further strength came from a galvanised steel capping plate that was held to the top of each door by rivets and pop rivets. Despite these

The inside of the door on this August 1949 model shows very clearly how the sidescreens bolt through the door tops and the canvas "triangle" gives access from outside to the door release mounted on the inside.

Each door has two sturdy galvanised hinges. The lower left-hand hinge is the same as the upper right-hand one, and vice versa.

reinforcements, door panels could fracture at their upper rear corners, and so from July 1950 Rover added a steel gusset plate on the inside of the affected area, just above the door latch on the inside of the door. This was attached by a combination of pop rivets and screws with nuts. Two galvanised hinges were bolted to the leading edge of each door, with their straight edges towards the upper and lower faces of the door and their angled edges facing one another.

The doors did not initially have any weather seals, although some were fitted from September 1949 (theoretically at chassis number 0610-1747) when Rover made an effort to improve the Land Rover's dust-proofing in a number of areas. These rubber weather seals were attached to the doors by retainer strips that were riveted in place.

There were never any door locks, and all 80-inch models had a simple latch arrangement at the top rear of each door. The latch and its handle were never painted, and on all the 1.6-litre models it was necessary to reach over the top of the door (through the sidescreen if fitted) to open it by using the handle inside. On the 1952 and 1953 (2-litre) models, simple sherardised external handles were fitted, and each door panel was drilled to allow the shank of its handle to pass through and into the back of the latch.

One very minor change was made to the later type of handle, when the rubber grommet that prevented the spindle of the handle chafing on the door panel was changed for a more effective type. This change took place in September 1952 at chassis numbers 3610-1070, 3613-0779, 3616-0652, 3630-0004, 3633-0005, 3636-0003, 3663-1331 and 3666-0289.

Wings

There were three different types of wing used on the 80-inch Land Rovers, and some sub-variants of these as well. The first type of wing was used on the first 1500 vehicles, up to December 1948, and was made of 14swg (2.032mm) Birmabright. The top, front, and inner valance formed a single assembly, and the outer side panel was bolted to this. These wings also had a cutaway section in the turned-over seam next to the radiator panel where they curved downwards, to ease the forming of the curve.

Interestingly, the first 150 or so vehicles had a sub-variant of this first wing type, where the both the right-hand and left-hand inner wing valances had cut-outs for the exhaust to pass through. The exhaust only ever passed through the left-hand valance, of course, but these early wings used a common valance pressing that was folded up to suit right-hand or left-hand wings as required. From L86-0181 in September 1948 (possibly at the same time), the inner wing valances changed slightly to make the exhaust easier to fit, and cover plates were screwed to their rear ends.

The second type of wing was made of thinner 16swg (1.626mm) sheet and did not have that cutaway in the seam because it could be more easily curved. The bolt-on side panel was otherwise unchanged, but there were changes to the top, front and inner valance pressing to suit the new pressed steel bulkhead. These wings were used up to and including chassis numbers 1610-3898, 1613-6865, 1616-3017, 1663-0078 and 1666-2022, and on all the 1951-season Station Wagons.

The third and final type of 80-inch wing was introduced on

A rubber buffer on each wing was designed to protect the panel from damage if the open door swung against it – although the panel around the buffer could dent quite easily if the door was opened hard against it.

Plenty of patina and no rubber buffer on the wing: this late Australian model was bought back by JLR Classic and went into their Land Rover Reborn programme.

the last 1.6-litre models, about a month before the end of the 1951 season. Here, the inner pressing was spot-welded to the outer panel, and the front of the wing was modified with a small peak or eyebrow pressed into the metal above a punched hole for the relocated sidelight.

On the first 2-litre models, built in late 1951, a problem developed with the front wings splitting in two places. Exactly why this occurred is not clear, but it would be surprising if it was not associated in some way with the installation of the 2-litre engine. One split occurred around the upper mounting hole for the grille panel and the Service modification was to rivet or bolt a reinforcing plate to the wing in the appropriate area. From approximately February 1952, such a plate was added to all wings on production. The second split occurred at the upper rear corner of the wing, and the Service fix was to make up a reinforcing plate and to attach it to the underside of the wing with two bolts.

Wings normally had a black rubber buffer just above the wheelarch, and this was designed to protect the panel from damage when the unrestrained door swung against it. For no immediately obvious reason, these buffers were often (perhaps always) omitted from 80-inch models built in Australia from CKD. The buffer of course also changed for the 1952 models,

The webbing protective strip and later style of oil recommendations panel are seen here on a 1950 model.

The later type of front panel is seen here on the 1953 AA vehicle. There are three cut-outs in the lower section and, as usual, two brackets to support the bottom of the grille.

to protect the wings against the new exterior door handles. Each wing also carried a sprung T-handle catch that was held in place by two bolts through a securing plate, and these catches engaged with staples on the bonnet to hold the bonnet closed.

Later models came as standard with a mirror bolted to the driver's side wing, and sometimes with one on each side. These mirrors were not fitted before the end of the 1951 season because they would reflect the bulkhead-mounted sidelights of the earlier models. The mirrors themselves were Lucas 540 types, like the earlier windscreen-mounted mirrors, and had a black body. They were mounted by an adjustable clamp to a cranked arm that bolted through the top surface of the wing.

Note that regulations concerning mirrors vary from country to country. In Britain, new regulations introduced in January 1958 affected Land Rovers, both existing and new, and these are summarised later on in connection with interior mirrors.

Front panel

The front panel to which the radiator grille and the radiator itself were fitted ran between the noses of the front wings and was set back in order to protect the headlights from vegetation in rural conditions. Like the rest of the bodywork, it was made of BB2 alloy.

There were two types of front panel on the 80-inch models. The first type was used on the "lights-behind" models and had three large rectangular openings in the upper part, plus a single narrower one that ran across the bottom. There were two brackets at the bottom to hold the bottom rail of the grille itself.

The second major type had a single central opening in the upper section, flanked by two circular cut-outs for the headlamps, and there were three smaller openings in the lower section. There were again two brackets at the bottom for the grille. This second type came in at chassis numbers 0611-1547 and 0620-0311, when the 7-inch headlamps (see below) were fitted. It remained unchanged when the inverted-T grille was introduced for the 1952 season.

All grille panels had a strip of khaki webbing attached to their tops by split rivets. This was intended to prevent the bonnet panel from chafing. On the horizontal top surface of each grille panel was a plate that listed recommended oils. Early plates were made of brass, and may have originally had a nickel silver and black finish. The later plates were made of alloy, had a very different style, and were printed in black. All plates were secured to the front panel by four drive screws.

Grille

The radiator grille was always made of galvanised thick steel wire that was woven to give a honeycomb pattern. Three different types of grille were used on the 80-inch Land Rover, and in each case an oval marque badge was bolted through the grille near the top to a metal plate behind. Details of the badges themselves are shown separately (below); their fixing bolts normally passed through the grille holes in the third row down from the top and the badge was located centrally.

The earliest type of grille, known as the "full" grille, had no cut-outs for the lights. Its bottom edge rested in two mounting plates welded to the front panel and its top edge was bolted to the grille panel through two brackets. There were three variants of the "full" grille, and in the period around late 1948 and early 1949, they were used more or less interchangeably as old stocks were used up on the assembly lines and newer types became available.

The earliest of these grilles had 27 squares at their widest point, with a missing top rail next to each fixing bracket. A

BODYWORK (LOWER)

The "full grille", with the headlamps behind the mesh, is seen here on a late 1949 model.

The second style of grille was introduced in mid-1950 and is known as the "lights-through" type.

This is the final "inverted T" style of grille, seen on a 1953 80-inch.

late variant of this grille, introduced probably in late November 1948 and used in parallel with the earlier type, does not have missing sections in the top rail. Then from approximately January 1949, the grilles were just 26 squares wide, with the missing sections of the top rail filled in. These later versions of the "full" grille were then fitted up to summer 1950.

The second type of grille was introduced with the larger 7-inch headlamps in May 1950 and is known as the "lights-through" type. This one had circular cut-outs that fitted around the headlamp rims, and was attached to the grille panel in the same way as the earlier type. It was introduced at chassis numbers 0611-1547 and 0621-0311, and remained in use for just over a year. It was then replaced by the third type of grille just before the start of the 1952 season and the changeover to 2-litre engines.

The third type of grille was very much simplified and was used on all the 2-litre models. It was made as an inverted T shape and fitted to the grille panel between the headlamps. Its bottom edge was retained in the same way as before but the top was retained by the bolts that passed through the oval Land Rover badge.

Bonnet

The bonnet panel was formed from a single sheet of Birmabright that was attached to a reinforcing frame of box sections formed from aluminium sheet. This reinforcing frame initially had two small cut-out sections where the fore-and-aft bracing struts fitted to it, but soon after the start of the 1950 model-year it was modified and the cut-out sections disappeared. The bonnet could be fitted with a carrier for the spare wheel, and this is described later under Optional Equipment.

Two galvanised steel hinges were bolted to the bonnet at the bulkhead end. Their other ends fitted into channels welded to the bulkhead, in a way that allowed the bonnet to be lifted off sideways to improve access to the engine. Also screwed to the bonnet on each side near the front was a small staple with a sherardised finish, which engaged with the bonnet catch mounted on the wing.

Bolted to the bonnet towards its front edge were two brackets that supported the windscreen frame when this was folded forwards. On some 1948 and 1949 models these were painted black, but other models had galvanised brackets. Each bracket was faced with a webbing buffer strip that was riveted in place. The clamps used to hold the folded windscreen in position were initially bolted to the bonnet itself and faced forwards, but from early January 1951 they were bolted to the windscreen support brackets and faced rearwards. This change took place at chassis numbers 1610-1483, 1613-2863, 1616-1318, 1630-0004, 1633-0004, 1636-0008, 1663-0043 and 1666-1423. At the same time, two small staples were bolted to the front of the bonnet on each side instead of the one on earlier vehicles. All these catches and bonnet fittings had a sherardised finish.

The bonnet prop rod was mounted on the left-hand inner wing (right-hand when looking into the engine bay). It was a simple but sturdy galvanised metal pole that swung up on a pivot bolted to the inner wing to engage with a slot on the underside of the bonnet frame. When not in use, it engaged with a spring clip on the inner wing panel. This spring clip was changed for a shorter one in March 1952 at chassis numbers 2610-4673, 2613-3129, 2616-2549, 2630-0007, 2633-0012, 2636-0005 and 2666-0973 – although it would be surprising if these changeover points recorded in the Parts Catalogue were absolute.

These two views of the bonnet show how the securing catches should lie. The August 1949 vehicle has its windscreen support brackets painted black, but the 1950 model shows the more common arrangement.

BODYWORK (LOWER)

The bonnet hinges were designed to enable easy removal of the bonnet itself for better access to the engine bay..

On the underside of this restored bonnet, the original finish has been faithfully re-created, the centre remaining in bare metal while there is a good deal of overspray at the sides.

These two pictures show minor differences in the construction of the bonnet frame. The light green one is the earlier; the discoloured one shows the simpler configuration adopted later in production.

69

The windscreen was always a two-pane type with a galvanised steel frame. This one is on an August 1949 model

The windscreen was designed to fold forwards onto the bonnet and to rest on two dedicated supports.

BODYWORK (LOWER)

The early mounting for the driver's mirror was a single bolt in the windscreen frame, as seen here on a November 1948 model.

Differences in the later windscreen frame are clear here, where the mirror mounting is quite different from the original type. Also clear here is the early type of mounting block for the optional trafficators, at the top of the screen rail.

Windscreen and frame

The two panes of screen glass were direct-glazed to a galvanised steel frame that pivoted on the bulkhead. The glass was plain and was not a safety type, although 80-inch models exported to the USA had to have laminated glass to meet regulations in place since 1936.

The windscreen frame was welded together from lengths of steel tube, and there was a flat vertical dividing bar in the centre. The first 500 or so vehicles had the same wide bar as the pre-production types, but all later ones had a narrower bar. The top rail of the frame had a series of hooks (known as "shark's teeth") welded to it, to take the metal loops at the front of the early canvas hoods. It also had sockets welded to its outer corners, to accept the hoodsticks when needed.

There was a Birmabright filler panel between the bottom rail of the frame and the bottom of the glass, and this was always painted in the body colour and retained by drive screws and pop rivets. A ventilator panel could be fitted in its place from June 1949, and this is described in the Optional Equipment section, later on. The bottom rail of the windscreen frame on the first 1500 Land Rovers had a rubber seal attached by drive screws with washers, but on later models the seal was relocated on the top of the bulkhead.

There were several other alterations to the windscreen frame in the first few years of production. They affected the bracket for the sidescreen hinges (see under Superstructure, in the next chapter), the mountings for the optional semaphore trafficators, and the mounting of the driver's mirror.

The earliest windscreen frames had no mountings for the trafficators or their control switch. They had a simple small bracket for the sidescreen hinges, about half-way up each vertical outer pillar, and a short cranked support arm for the

71

When a mounting bracket for the optional trafficator control switch was added, it was initially offset towards the driver's side, as here.

"handed", windscreen assemblies.

The next major change was at chassis number 86-1501 about a month later. There were new and much larger triangular brackets for the sidescreen hinges, each with a drilled hole in the forward end. The support arm for the driver's mirror, now longer than before, was bolted through this. The mirror itself remained unchanged.

A further change had taken place by the autumn of 1949 and this time improved the trafficator mounting arrangements. On the inside of the screen assembly, the bracket for the control switch was relocated to the centre so that the same assembly could be used for both LHD and RHD models, and on the outside, the trafficator brackets changed from block types to triangular ones.

At the start of the 1952 season, the driver's mirror was removed from the windscreen, and in its place there was a mirror mounted on the front wing. The sidescreen hinge brackets nevertheless retained the drilled hole through which the mirror arm had been mounted on earlier models.

The windscreen frame was arranged to pivot forwards and to rest on supports mounted on the bonnet. There was a pivot eye at the bottom of each side element of the frame, and a bolt through each one went into the bulkhead. As usual, the precise arrangements evolved over the years, and there were three different versions of the pivot bolt arrangement.

On the earliest models, each pivot bolt had a castle nut with a split pin. This arrangement was used up to mid-April 1950. At chassis number 0611-0749, a simpler arrangement was introduced, with the pivot bolt held only by a split pin. However, this proved unsatisfactory and was discontinued before the end of the 1950 season. Its lasting replacement, introduced at chassis number 0611-5324, was a special locking nut on the end of each pivot bolt. All three arrangements were sometimes accompanied by washers on the pivot pin to provide a better fit: this was very necessary because the tolerances could vary by as much as 3/8 inch!

When erected, the windscreen frame was held in place by two clamp-type fasteners. These were attached to bosses on the inside face of the frame's bottom rail and hooked over brackets on the bulkhead. The original clamps had straight arms, but curved arms were introduced late in 1950, at chassis numbers 1610-1420, 1613-2794, 1616-1310, 1630-0004, 1633-0004, 1636-0008, 1663-0043 and 1666-1507. (Note that this change seems to have been accidentally omitted from some editions of the Parts Catalogue.)

An interior driving mirror was never fitted as standard to the 80-inch models. Rover introduced one for the Land Rover in summer 1956 (the June 1956 Service Bulletin announces it), and it was possible to retro-fit this to an 80-inch model. This mirror was attached to the top windscreen rail by two drive screws, and it was not positioned in the centre above the dividing bar but to the left of centre on LHD models and to the right of centre on RHD models.

standard driving mirror was bolted through the driver's side pillar. The mirror was a Lucas 540 type (with Lucas part number 062561), which had a circular body with a black finish.

The first changes occurred at chassis number 86-0750 in November 1948. At this point, Rover added mountings for the optional trafficators (see Optional Equipment). These were a tapped block welded to the top of each outer windscreen rail to accept the trafficator itself, and a bracket for the control switch welded to the inner edge of the frame's bottom rail. The control switch bracket was initially offset towards the driver's side, which meant that Rover had to produce two different,

LAND ROVER BADGES

A Land Rover oval badge was always displayed on the radiator grille at the front of the vehicle and on the tail panel at the rear. The rear badge was on the left-hand side on vehicles with right-hand drive but on the right-hand side for left-hand-drive vehicles.

The very first pre-production Land Rovers had no badges at all, as confirmed by pictures of L05 at the Amsterdam Show in 1948. However, a distinctive oval badge was soon designed, and was initially cast from brass, with a width of 5½ inches. On pre-production models, the rim was flat, but the production type had a raised rim. There are several schools of thought about the way these badges were painted – and the pre-production type may not have been painted at all.

It is probable that some very early production badges had red letters and a red rim on a black background, those two colours matching the major colours on the Viking ship badge used on Rover saloons. At some point in 1948, probably over the summer, a change was then made to a Light Green background (to match the body colour), while retaining the red letters and red rim.

A surviving drawing confirms approval of a further colour change on 29 November 1948. The red of the letters and rim was replaced by yellow and, assuming the change took a few weeks to filter through to production, it is reasonable to assume that the new colours were in use by early 1949.

However, these yellow-on-Light Green badges lasted for only a few months because, in summer 1949, the body colour changed from Light Green to Deep Bronze Green. The background colour changed to match, so that the definitive 80-inch badges had yellow lettering and rim against a Deep Bronze Green background. These lasted until the summer of 1951.

The cast brass badges were probably expensive to produce, and for the 1952 and later models Rover changed to a simpler badge that was pressed from light alloy sheet. This badge was larger, with a width of 7 3/16 inches, and the Land Rover emblem and rim were in plain metal while the background was painted black. The legend, "Birmingham, England", was also added in smaller letters.

All these badges had two fixing holes. On the grille, slot-head screws attached the badge, passing through the grille and a plate behind it, with securing nuts concealed behind that. On the tail panel, the badge was secured by two screws.

This red-on-light green badge probably superseded the original red-on-black type. (Jochen von Arnim)

Next came yellow on light green, in early 1949. (Jochen von Arnim)

From summer 1949, the background of the badge changed to match the new Bronze Green body colour.

From autumn 1951, this pressed aluminium badge replaced the earlier cast type. Note that it reads "Birmingham"; the similar type of badge reading "Solihull" was not introduced until much later. (Jochen von Arnim)

No.2 Green
Deep Bronze Green
Fire Engine Red
Light Stone
L1 Green
L2 Blue
L3 Grey
L4 Beige

PAINT OPTIONS

There was no choice of body paint colour for the first three or so years of Land Rover production, although a small number of vehicles would have been painted to special order (see below). The standard paints on 80-inch models were as follows:

To May 1949 (approx)
Light Green, also known as **"No2 Green"**, this green being the second colour listed for the Rover P3 saloons of the time. The ICI paint code for this colour is 2602 and the Herbert's code is 00778.

From June 1949 (approx)
Dark Green, also known as **Deep Bronze Green** or simply as **Bronze Green**. It was the standard "peacetime" colour for all British military vehicles and was required for the 1878 Land Rovers whose delivery to the War Department began in summer 1949. Rover decided to standardise the colour on civilian vehicles as well at the same time, and a contributory factor may have been that No2 Green was to be discontinued for Rover cars over the summer. The ICI paint code for Deep Bronze Green is 2651, and the Herbert's code is 00428; some suppliers understand the code BS381C-224 better.

Rover was never afraid to entertain special orders. In late 1949 and early 1950, quite large numbers of 0610-series chassis were painted **Black** and were shipped to the Crown Agents in Malaya – perhaps intended for police duties.

Alternative paint colours began to appear in the 1952 season. Military orders were again a major reason: the War Department asked for 850 vehicles from a major contract that was then going down the assembly lines to be delivered in **Light Stone** for service in the Middle East. The Royal Navy had its vehicles delivered in **dark blue**, and the RAF had some of its vehicles delivered in its characteristic **blue-grey**. From May 1952, Fire Engines were delivered in **red**.

From November 1952, for export vehicles only and apparently beginning with chassis 3610-1721, the colour range consisted of **Beige, Blue** and **Grey** in addition to the standard **Dark Green**. The season's four colours were now listed in the Despatch Department's records with numbers. They were
L1 Green
L2 Blue (= RAF Blue)
L3 Grey
L4 Beige.

Details for the **Ivory** paint used on hardtops and Truck Cabs will be found in the next chapter. Land Rover paints in this period had a gloss finish (although the paint was typically allowed to weather to a dull finish), and they could be buffed to give a good shine if the owner so wished.

BODYWORK (UPPER) & CANVAS

This chapter looks at all the superstructure that was available for the basic Land Rover – the sidescreens, the canvas roofs, and the metal roofs. As far as the Rover Company was concerned, all types of Land Rover roof were production options and were therefore listed in the optional equipment section of the parts catalogues. An honourable exception was made for the sidescreens (even though they were an extra-cost option before October 1948), which became considered as part of the basic vehicle and were listed in the main section of the catalogues.

For convenience, all these elements of the superstructure are considered together here rather than in the chapter on Optional Equipment.

SIDESCREENS

There were two types of sidescreen (door top), one with an access flap to suit the doors with no handles, and the other with no flap to suit the later doors with exterior handles. All sidescreens had a fixed front window and a sliding rear one, with galvanised frames and a large rectangular Birmabright filler plate in their lower half that was painted in the body colour and riveted in place (the rivets were added through the painted panel and were therefore unpainted). The sidescreens fitted to the doors by means of two long rods that passed through holes in the top of each door. Their threaded ends were then fixed in place with nuts.

Sidescreens were one of the extra-cost options for the first few months of Land Rover production, but became standard equipment in October 1948. The early ones (on 1.6-litre models) had a triangular canvas flap riveted to the rear edge of the filler plate, and access to the door latch from outside was through this. The later ones did not have this canvas flap, because the door could be opened from the outside with a handle. Riveted to each flap was a short metal strip that helped keep them closed.

All sidescreens had the same weather sealing, which consisted of a rubber draught strip at the front (attached by upper and lower retaining strips), a large canvas flap at the rear, and a rubber draught strip on the lower edge to form a seal between the sidescreen and the top of the door. On early

The early type of hinge for the sidescreens was this flimsy-looking Y-shaped type.

models these lower strips were attached by 11 drive screws and washers, but from 86-2501 in December 1949 nine spring clips did the job and no doubt saved time in production.

Both the fixed front window and the sliding rear one were mounted in channels within the sidescreen. Each channel originally had two separate retainers, but a simpler design attached by screws was used from chassis number 866-6250 in 1949; at the same time, an end piece for the window channel was added to each door top. Both windows were always made of Perspex. The sliding panes had a lozenge-shaped finger-cut out in their leading edges until early February 1952, when the cut-out was deleted and a Perspex knob was bonded to the inside of the window instead. At the same time, the sliding panes gained aluminium frames and an aluminium trim piece was added to the trailing edge of each fixed pane. This change took place at chassis numbered 2610-3085, 2613-2971, 2616-2028, 2663-0224 and 2666-0427, and is another one not recorded in the Parts Catalogue.

Sidescreens were hinged from the windscreen frame, and there were three different types of hinge. On all 1.6-litre models except for the last few thousand in 1951, the hinge

FACTORY-ORIGINAL LAND ROVER SERIES I, 80-INCH MODELS

The canvas strips attached to the rear uprights of the sidescreens close over the canvas of the hood, as here.

The sliding panes of the early sidescreens had a simple finger cut-out in their leading edges.

Late sidescreens had a finger grip; this one is on a 1953 model.

was made of thick wire bent into a Y-shape. These hinges were prone to breakage, and Rover later made a repair kit available, consisting of a bolt-on hinge with an adaptor plate.

From late May 1951, a more robust hinge with a flat triangular plate was used. This was introduced at chassis numbers 1610-3311, 1613-5971, 1616-2551, 1630-0004, 1633-0007, 1636-0009, 1663-0078 and 1666-1974. There was then a third type of hinge that was introduced in late June 1952 at chassis numbers 2610-5443, 2613-5779, 2616-3456, 2630-0014, 2636-0005, 2663-1953 and 2666-1021. This final type of hinge was essentially the same as the second type but allowed for a degree of fore and aft adjustment.

In October 1953, Service literature flagged up a problem with early sidescreen brackets fracturing, and recommended their replacement with the latest type of bracket in cases of need.

CANVAS ROOFS

Rover followed the lead of the wartime Jeep in using canvas for the superstructure of the Land Rover. This provided basic weather protection and was relatively cheap and easy to obtain as Land Rover production started up in the late 1940s. It was a way of saving precious supplies of metal – rationed through the Ministry of Supply – so that Rover's allocation could be used to produce a greater quantity of vehicles.

The canvas used for the hoods and parts of the sidescreens was a military grade. High-quality modern reproductions of these items have been available for many years, some with improved modern materials that resist shrinkage better than the original canvas and are virtually indistinguishable from it. It is worth knowing that there have also been other products that have not followed the original specification very closely. For a note on colour, see the sidebar on page 83.

Very early 80-inch models could be had with a detachable canvas cover for the cab area as standard and this is generally known as the "three-seater" hood. It was supplemented by what Rover called the "seven-seater" hood that covered the cab and the back body, and from October 1948 this became standard equipment for some markets, including Britain. The three-seater hood remained available but there was little demand for it and it was discontinued when stocks were exhausted during 1950.

Interestingly, these descriptions were changed when Rover realised that the reference to seats left them open to accusations that the vehicle was capable of carrying passengers and was therefore not exempt from Purchase Tax as a commercial vehicle! So by April 1950 the two types were known as the "driver's" hood and the "full-length" hood.

The sidescreens can be completely removed. These two are the 1952-1953 pattern, with finger grips glued to the inner surfaces of the sliding panes and plate-type hinges.

The three-seater hood covered only the driving compartment. Note the gauze "windows" in this example.

Three-seater hood and sticks

The three-seater hood was supported on a detachable framework that consisted of three parts. The main one was a hooped hood stick that fitted into sockets in the cappings at the front of the back body. This was then braced to the windscreen frame by two tie-rods that fitted into the hoodstick sockets on the frame. Everything was secured by wing nuts.

The canvas came in two sections. One formed the roof and rear quarters of the cab, and the other was a rear curtain. The roof section had metal loops at its front edge, and these hooked over the "shark's teeth" on the windscreen top rail. One strap on each side then held the roof to the supporting tie-rods, and two long webbing straps with dull-finish metal buckles held the rear of the roof to the front edge of the body tub. Each rear quarter panel also had three quick-release fasteners along its leading edge.

The rear curtain incorporated a pair of rectangular "windows" to enable the driver to see behind the vehicle. These were made out of fine-mesh brass gauze with a greenish khaki appearance. The curtain had five reinforced slots at the top for fixing straps, and three loops on each side; the webbing straps between roof and body tub were threaded through these to hold the curtain in position.

Full hood and sticks

The full hood was supported by two identical hooped sticks. One fitted into the sockets at the front of the body, exactly as for the three-seater hood, and the other fitted into sockets at the rear corners of the body. These two hoops were then braced to one another by a tubular tie rod on each side, attached just below the radius of the hoodstick by bolts and wing nuts.

There was a change in the design of the hoodsticks from January 1950. Early ones had a horizontal top section, but this allowed water and debris to collect on the hood canvas and to cause it to rot. The later sticks had a pronounced curvature at the top that gave an arched profile to the canvas roof and allowed water to drain from it. This change was made at chassis numbers 0610-5463 and 0630-0027.

There were also three types of full-length hood. All of them had webbing straps and buckles on the inside that held them

FACTORY-ORIGINAL LAND ROVER SERIES I, 80-INCH MODELS

Hoods of all types are secured by the row of "shark's teeth" along the windscreen top rail. This was the early type of fixing, with brass loops.

to the hood sticks. The first type was used up to summer 1949, the second up to the end of that year, and the third on all subsequent models.

The earliest type of hood (sometimes known as "loop and strap" type) had two short leather straps sewn to the bottom of each side panel and two long webbing straps sewn to the rear roof valance. The side straps passed through the staples on the body sides and the rear straps passed through the staples on the tail panels. The long rear straps also had leather strap guards to prevent them fretting against the panels on either side of the tailboard. Several metal loops were sewn into the front of the roof section, and these hooked over the "shark's teeth" on the windscreen header rail. These first hoods had a detachable rear curtain, with three loops stitched to each side; the long webbing straps had to be detached from the staples on the body and threaded through these when the curtain was fitted. The curtain also had two rectangular rear windows made out of the fine-mesh brass gauze that was used for the windows of the three-seater hood.

The second type of hood was introduced in summer 1949, theoretically at chassis number 866-6001 in May. The major change was that the hood was now attached by rope (and fitting or removing it was therefore much easier and quicker than before). Rope was threaded through the lower edges of the canvas, and emerged in six places (two on each side and two at the rear) to fit over the cleats now welded to the bodywork. The use of rope for fixing gave this second type of hood one of its nicknames, which is the "bootlace" type.

The metal loops for the windscreen header rail were now replaced by a webbing strip that tucked under the shark's teeth on the header rail. The rear curtain was now permanently stitched to the rear roof valance, and although it still had two rectangular windows, these were now made of heavy celluloid. The curtain was laced to the sides of the main hood through eight reinforced eyelet holes in a zig-zag pattern (which gives this version of the hood its alternative nickname of "zig-zag hood"). The rope used to secure this second type of hood had a length of 90 inches – or 99 inches, according to some parts catalogues.

The third and final type of 80-inch hood was introduced in December 1949 at chassis numbers 0610-5463 and 0630-0028, and was designed to go with the arched hoodsticks. Its most obvious feature was that the rear curtain now had extension "wings" that wrapped round the sides of the main hood, while the hood itself had a pocket at the rear on each side and a buckle just ahead of this. The "wings" of the rear curtain had to be tucked into these pockets, and the short webbing strap attached to each one had to be pulled out of the other end of the pocket and attached to the buckle. This third type of hood could also be fitted optionally with a partition or fume curtain (see the Optional Equipment chapter). The rear curtain had to be laced shut with rope, as on the second type of hood, and the length of rope required for this was 56 inches.

Worth noting is that replacement hoods supplied by Rover after about 1954 had a single Perspex rear window instead of the two rectangular windows. This change appears to have been made in anticipation of new legal requirements governing visibility to the rear of the vehicle.

The later hoods – this is on an August 1949 model – had a simpler form of fixing without the brass loops.

BODYWORK (UPPER) & CANVAS

The structure formed by the hood sticks was the same throughout 80-inch production, although there was a difference between the flat-topped sticks seen here and the later arched sticks.

On this August 1949 model, the lacing of the hood securing rope can be seen. The rope is secured to the Y-shaped lashing attachments next to the corner cappings. Meanwhile, the two long webbing straps pass through staples on the cappings next to the tailgate.

Like the three-seater hood, the first type of rear curtain featured fine-mesh gauze rather than transparent plastic in its "windows". The strap-type fixings are very clear here.

FACTORY-ORIGINAL LAND ROVER SERIES I, 80-INCH MODELS

The rear curtain rolls up and can be secured in the open position with its own webbing straps.

The buckles along the upper sides of the hood can be used to secure the side canvas sections in the open position.

The rope-type hood fixing passed through cleats welded to the body sides.

The wrap-around sides of the third type of hood can be clearly seen on this 1953 model.

METAL ROOFS

The earliest known drawing for what Rover called the Detachable Metal Top is dated March 1950, and shows that it was intended from the beginning to be available with or without side windows: the window on the drawing is clearly labelled "side lights to special order". The two types are now generally described as hardtop and window hardtop.

The earliest known sales leaflet for the Truck Cab option is dated June 1952, although some experts believe the option was made available for export earlier; the sales leaflet itself also shows the Truck Cab on a 1951 model. It was suitable for 80-inch models of all types, and was certainly retro-fitted to some older vehicles.

Hardtop (and window hardtop)

The window hardtop actually became available before the plain hardtop, in about spring 1950, and the earliest sales brochure for option E7 was issued that April. All the first examples went for export, where demand was probably greater anyway. By combining the window hardtop with the inward-facing rear bench seats already available, it was possible to create a

BODYWORK (UPPER) & CANVAS

Uncharacteristically, this early window hardtop has its galvanised corner cappings painted. The side windows and that in the "cat flap" were rubber-glazed.

This view of one of the first hardtop 80-inch models for the Post Office shows the key features of the metal roof, with galvanised corner plates that butted up to those on the body tub and a top-hinged "cat flap" above the tailboard.
(Post Office Archives)

In this case, the "cat flap" is open and supported on its two sprung quadrant arms.
(Post Office Archives)

rather crude form of station wagon. In Britain, however, only the hardtop with plain sides was made available, because Rover were very sensitive to any suggestion that the Land Rover might be used for carrying passengers, which would make it liable to Purchase Tax.

The window hardtop was an aluminium alloy structure with a glazed fixed window in each side, a top-hinged flap at the rear with a further glazed window, and a roof with angled front section and external ribs for reinforcement. The opening top section, familiarly known as a "cat flap", had a sprung quadrant at each side to support it in the open position. The whole hardtop assembly was attached to existing points on the host vehicle by bolts and wing nuts. The April 1950 sales brochure stated that the hardtop was available only in Cream – but actually showed what may have been a prototype that was in the same colour as the Land Rover to which it was mounted. The colour described as "Cream" was actually Ivory; see below.

The earliest evidence of the plain-sided "van" hardtop being available dates from autumn 1950, when the Post Office took the first of several 1951 models for its Telephones division. Nevertheless, the plain hardtop remained quite rare on the 80-inch Land Rover. It came with the same "cat flap" at the rear as the window hardtop.

Window hardtops for export were often fitted with a Tropical Roof, a second alloy panel bolted to the outside of the roof and also painted Ivory. It was secured by several bolts with distance pieces, and rested on the three stiffening ribs at the front of the cab section. The theory was that the air gap between the two panels would allow air to circulate, so reducing the amount of heat transmitted into the vehicle body – an important consideration when the window hardtop was being used as a passenger-carrier. The Tropical Roof was a simple but successful design that was carried over to the Station Wagons introduced on the 86-inch chassis in 1953, and would remain in production for Land Rovers for another 30 years.

After the Station Wagon model ended production in mid-1951, the absence of a window hardtop from the options list in Britain meant that no passenger-carrying option was available from the factory. This provided an opportunity for aftermarket suppliers, and it appears that Ernest Battley Ltd of Coventry made at least one example of a metal hardtop

The metal cab roof is seen here on a 1953 fire engine, for which it was an optional extra. The ladder supports were obviously not fitted to standard cabs. The canvas flap at the back of the sidescreen served to cover the large gap between sidescreen and cab rear panel.

with glazed windows in the sides and tail. This came with a full-height tail door that had a spare wheel carrier on its outer face. The introduction of a new Station Wagon on the 86-inch chassis for the 1954 season must have left no market for this conversion, and it is not clear how many were ever made. The Battley company subsequently specialised in making up-and-over garage doors.

Truck Cab

In conjunction with the sidescreens, the Truck Cab provided a (reasonably) weather-proof driving compartment without compromising access to the back body. It was normally painted in Ivory, but was red on fire engines.

The Truck Cab consisted of two main sections, both made of Birmabright BB2. The roof was one section; it sloped forwards and was braced on the outside by three stiffening ribs running front to rear. The other section was the vertical rear panel, which incorporated small side extensions and a large rectangular window with two sliding Perspex sections. Each sliding section had a metal reinforcement at its edge (in the centre of the aperture), and there was a simple hook-type catch to secure the window closed. Each of the side extensions was reinforced at its bottom edge by a galvanised metal plate riveted in place.

The rear panel was attached to the body by long studs that fitted into the forward hoodstick sockets, and had a reinforcing piece of angled metal at its base. The roof had rubber seals attached all round its underside, with additional rubber mounting blocks and draught-excluder blocks in each rear corner. It was attached by bolts to the rear panel and by

BODYWORK (UPPER) & CANVAS

The front edge of the cab roof was protected by a galvanised capping. One of the strengthening ribs is also visible here.

COLOURS: CANVAS AND METAL TOPS

Canvas tops
The canvas used for the original hoods of 80-inch Land Rovers was always khaki, and of course matched the canvas used for the flaps in the early sidescreens.

Metal tops
Rover chose a light colour for the panels of the Hardtop and the roof of the Truck Cab "to assist the interior cooling of the driving compartment when the Land-Rover is being used in hot climates," as a sales leaflet for the Truck Cab explained it.

This colour was initially described as "cream" in Service and Sales literature, but was actually known as Ivory and has ICI paint code 2155 and Herbert's code 0416.

Although Ivory was the standard colour for these metal roofs, Rover would also paint them to order – for example, when a customer had the vehicle painted in a special livery and wanted the top panels to match it.

clamps to the hood stay brackets on the windscreen top rail. The Truck Cab also came with a distance piece for the spare wheel mounting, designed to prevent the wheel from fretting against the rear panel of the cab.

For export, the Truck Cab could be supplied with a Tropical Roof. This was a short version of the Tropical Roof panel available for the window hardtop body (see above), and like that one was also painted Ivory. It was secured by six bolts with distance pieces, and rested on the three stiffening ribs.

The rear panel of the metal cab was held in place by large pins that passed through the hoodstick sockets and by a bolted angle bracket.

ELECTRICAL ITEMS

All standard 80-inch Land Rovers had a 12-volt electrical system with a positive earth. The system was very simple and as a result had minimal fuse arrangements. The battery was charged by an engine-driven dynamo and a constant voltage control arrangement was incorporated. All components were manufactured by Lucas.

Note that the SU electric fuel pump is covered in the earlier chapter on the Engine.

Battery

The battery was always fitted in the engine compartment, on a dedicated platform at the right front of the chassis (left side when standing looking into the engine compartment). Original-equipment batteries would have had black rubber casings, and were rated at 51ah. Clamp-type terminal connections were fitted to the wiring. The feed cable was sheathed in black plastic but the earth cable was a braided strap without any outer sheath.

Wiring harness

The wiring harness always had an outer sheath of black cotton braid, with a green and brown fleck stripe running through it, although that stripe is often hard to see on the exposed parts of an elderly harness. The cables inside are braided and lacquered.

Few things spoil the look of a restored engine bay more than an incorrect modern battery. The original type can still be bought, and is seen here. Also visible on this 1.6-litre engine are the side-entry distributor cap, the correct style of wiring harness with its flecked braid covering, an SU fuel pump complete with the original style of labelling, and the control box with its wires correctly and neatly located.

Top-quality reproduction wiring harnesses have been available for several years, and some suppliers will incorporate custom modifications for such things as flashing direction indicators.

There were minor variations of detail from one harness to the next, to suit the electrical equipment fitted, and there were five basic types. Military vehicles and some export models (such as those for the USA) also had special variations to suit their special lighting installations. A change in the harness securing arrangements occurred at chassis number 0610-2501 (approximately) because some harnesses had become trapped between the floor of the body and the chassis cross-member. Three securing clips were reversed to locate the harness safely below the top of the cross-member, and at the same time the rear corners of the floor stiffeners were angled to give additional clearance. This change was also recommended as a Service modification for existing vehicles.

Visible changes during the 80-inch production run included the addition of a 3ft length of plastic insulating tube over the headlamp cable harness at chassis number 0610-4001 in November 1949, intended to protect the wiring from spilled battery acid. There were also small pressed metal covers on early vehicles, to protect the harness where it passed through the chassis frame, but later models used circular rubber grommets instead.

Control box and fuses

Rover considered that the electrical system was simple enough to be safe with a single fuse on most models, although at one period 80-inch Land Rovers were being fitted with two fuses. These fuses were always cartridge types.

There were three different arrangements for the control box and fuses over the years. The first arrangement lasted until late December 1949, and consisted of a separate voltage control box and fuse box mounted on a metal plate that was in turn bolted to the engine side of the bulkhead on the right-hand side (left side when looking into the engine compartment). The control box was a Lucas RF96/2 L13, with a black Bakelite cover that was retained by a wire that clipped over it. The fuse box was a Lucas SF5/2, also made from black Bakelite, and contained a single 25-amp fuse.

The second arrangement had no separate fuse box, but the control box itself had provision for two fuses. This was introduced at chassis numbers 0610-6035 and 0620-0140. The control box was now a Lucas RF95/2 L2, with nine terminals. The body of the unit was made of black Bakelite, and the two 35-amp fuses were carried up against the terminal block. There were clips for two spare fuses on the body of the unit. This type of control box was mounted to a smaller plate on the bulkhead, in much the same place as the earlier type.

The third arrangement was introduced in late June 1951, and reverted to the earlier arrangement with a separate control box and fuse box. The two were again mounted on a large plate that was bolted to the bulkhead. This arrangement was introduced at chassis numbers 1610-3899, 1613-6866, 1616-3018, 1663-0079 and 1666-2023. It was carried over to the 2-litre models and remained unchanged until 80-inch production ended.

The control box was a Lucas RB106/1, which as usual had a black Bakelite cover. The fuse box was again an SF5/2, and its single fuse was a 35-amp type on 1.6-litre models but a 25-amp type on 2-litre types.

All these electrical components were shared with other vehicles of the period, and modern reproductions have been made available.

Dynamo

The dynamo was belt-driven from the crankshaft pulley, and shared its belt (the "fan belt") with the water pump. It was always mounted on an adjustable bracket on the right of the engine (left when looking into the engine compartment).

Three different types were used over the years, all being variants of the Lucas C39P type. The earliest type was a plain C39P, with solid end plates and a plain pulley, and this was used until approximately June 1949. The front end plate and main body were black but the rear end plate was unpainted.

It gave way to the self-cooled type C39PV, which had ventilated ends and fan blades on the pulley. The third type was then introduced well into the 1953 season, at engine numbers 3610-8386 and 3613-7385. This was a type C39P2LO, had a slightly higher output, and was again ventilated. The ventilated ends of these two were always unpainted.

The mounting flange, rear clamp, top bracket and adjustment bracket were never painted on any of these dynamos.

The correct type of wiring harness, with flecked braided cotton cover, is seen here on a 1948 model. The electrical connections to the control box alongside are neat, as they would have been when new.

The starter motor on a 1948 model.

On very early vehicles, the coil had these knurled Bakelite knob fixings.

Starter motor

The starter motor was always a Lucas M418G, but there were two different types. Both had a black body but the exposed end, clamp ring and the circular housing that bolted to the flywheel housing were unpainted. Some have nevertheless been found with black clamp rings.

The first variant of the starter motor was type M418G/76, but this was replaced in the early part of 1949 by an M418G/C. Theoretically, the changeover took place at engine number 86-2235, but in practice the two types seem to have overlapped with one another on the assembly lines. Reconditioned examples are not hard to find today.

Distributor, ignition leads, and spark plugs

Both 1.6-litre and 2-litre engines had a DVXH4A distributor. (Note that early Lucas lists incorrectly listed a DVXH6A.) This had the usual unpainted alloy lower body and a Bakelite cap in black (sometimes brown). This was a side-entry distributor, with the ignition leads emerging horizontally. Reconditioned distributors are fairly easily available, as are the bushes and springs necessary for DIY refurbishment.

All ignition leads were originally black. Those running to the spark plugs had conical black plastic shrouds with a sealing ring at the cylinder head end and a knurled plastic nut at the top to secure the plug lead. It was possible for condensation to form in the spark plug covers, leading to misfires, and so to cure this in June 1950 Rover recommended dealers to drill four 3/16in holes in each cover – and to align the covers carefully so that the holes allowed an airflow from front to rear as the vehicle was in motion!

Original equipment spark plugs were initially Lodge HL14P or HLNR types, and then Lodge CLN from March 1952. Suppressors were an option (see Optional Equipment chapter).

Coil

The coil was a Lucas B12 type on both 1.6-litre and 2-litre models and was always mounted to the bulkhead, just to the left of centre (right when looking into the engine compartment). Its top pointed away from the centre of the vehicle. Very early examples had knurled Bakelite knobs on threaded terminals, but most of those fitted to 80-inch Land Rovers had nut fastenings.

Most coils had simple nut fixings on the terminals. This one has been refurbished in the correct black finish.

Horn

There was a single horn, bolted behind the grille panel. All the 1.6-litre models and the early 2-litres had a Lucas Altette HF1235 type with an offset adjuster. The later 2-litres, from chassis number 2610-4737, had a later version of the same horn, this time with a central adjuster. These horns were stamped with the date of their manufacture.

The wiring to the horn passed through a junction box that was screwed to the left-hand inner wing. This junction box was a round Lucas 6J type made of black Bakelite.

Windscreen wiper

Only one windscreen wiper was standard on the 80-inch Land Rovers. It was mounted on the driver's side and was powered by a Lucas CW1 motor that was bolted to the inside of the windscreen frame. The motor body had a crackle-black finish and its control levers were unpainted. The power cable for the motor was armoured and was exposed outside the bulkhead on all models built before early May 1950. Then from chassis number 0611-1546 the cable was re-routed through an extra hole in the bulkhead above the steering column, and the armouring was no longer needed.

A second motor could be fitted as an option to the passenger's side, and was identical to the first, with the same wiring arrangements but in mirror-image to suit the opposite side of the vehicle.

The wiper arm was another Lucas product, and there were two types. On early motors, the arm was secured to the wiper motor spindle by a nut, but on later ones the arm was a push-fit onto a serrated spindle.

The CW1 wiper motor was used on several other vehicles at the time of the 80-inch and was first introduced during the 1930s. Demand for replacements has ensured that parts to repair these motors are fairly readily available, although it is important to note that there were 6-volt types as well as the 12-volt type used on the 80-inch Land Rover.

Note that no 80-inch Land Rover was ever built with any form of windscreen washer system. However, as windscreen washers have become a legal requirement in most countries, owners have fitted a variety of systems.

The wiper arm was secured to the earliest type of motor by a nut on the end of the spindle. This is on a 1948 model.

Push-fit wiper blades were used on later models, like this one on a 1950 vehicle. The brass colour on the arm was not standard.

Lighting

Lighting can be a problematical area for restorers because lighting regulations have changed over the years, and in some cases modern regulations make strict originality illegal for road use. Lighting regulations also differ from country to country, and all restorers should check what is permissible in their own country before deciding on how to restore the lighting system on an early Land Rover.

As examples, it is interesting to list three difficulties that restorers face in Britain. The first is that the early 80-inch models, up to chassis number 0611-2000, had wiring configured to extinguish the right-hand headlamp when the left-hand lamp was dipped. The law now requires double-dipping headlamps, where both lamps remain lit on dipped beam (a specification that was always used on export models of the Land Rover from the beginning). The second is that direction indicators were never standard on an 80-inch, but British law now requires that all vehicles built after 1936 should have them. The third is that the 1953 Road Transport Lighting Act required two red reflectors of a minimum size to be fitted to the rear of all vehicles after 1st October 1954, and was retrospective in its effect; early Land Rovers had no reflectors at all.

Headlamps

The 80-inch Land Rovers had two different types of headlamp, the early ones being tractor types with a 5-inch diameter and the later ones car types with a 7-inch diameter.

The 5-inch headlamps were used on all early models, where the headlamps were protected behind the radiator grille. They were made by Butler, of Small Heath in Birmingham, a company which was bought out by Lucas during 1948. Lucas continued to market many of the Butler products, which were

The "lights behind" configuration seen here on an August 1949 model always used 5-inch Butler headlamps.

Later models, like this 1953 2-litre that formerly belonged to the AA, again had Lucas F700 7-inch headlamps.

Unique to the 1951 model-year was this arrangement, with Lucas F700 7-inch headlights emerging through shaped sections in the grille.

well established with (among others) tractor manufacturers, and gave their own product code of L-WD-HO to these headlamps. The lamps had a black metal body, fluted glass, and a 36-watt output on both main and dipped beams. The mounting bolt was on top of the lamp body. In Britain, a single-filament bulb was used in the right-hand headlamp to suit the early dipping system which required the offside headlamp to be extinguished. All later headlamps and all export headlamps from the beginning had double-filament bulbs.

From early May 1950, the headlamps changed to car-type units with a 7-inch diameter. The changeover points are shown above in the section on the Grille, which was changed at the same time to accommodate them. These new lamps were Lucas F700 types, with block-pattern lenses, a 42-watt output on main beam but the same 36-watt output on dipped beam. They were screwed to the grille panel through their rims, which were in body colour on 1951 models but could be either body colour or chromed on the 1952-1953 2-litre models (although the chrome was painted over on military vehicles to prevent reflections).

Lenses for right-hand-drive and left-hand-drive models differed, to suit the different dipping requirements, and there were some other minor variations, such as yellow bulbs to meet the regulations then in force in France.

The F700 lamps remained unchanged when the inverted-T pattern grill replaced the "lights-through" type on 1952 models, even though the new grille did give a very different appearance to the front of the Land Rover.

Sidelamps

The first Land Rovers had sidelights mounted on the bulkhead, but this arrangement did cause some problems. The lights were not compatible with wing-mounted mirrors because they reflected in them at night, and in some countries (the USA was

Bulkhead-mounted sidelamps on the early models had frosted lenses.

The sockets for the bulkhead-mounted sidelamps were covered by a blanking plate on Land Rovers for North America.

The standard original-equipment tail lamp unit was the Lucas ST51/1, understandably known as the D-lamp.

In Britain, Rover recommended this very similar-looking Lucas lamp (without the bar across the lens) to meet new regulations introduced in 1956. Here it is fitted to a 1949 Land Rover that was then still in service with the Derby Fire Brigade. The rear reflector met changing regulations, but in this case was not mounted in the position recommended by the factory.

one example) they did not meet local regulations that governed the position of side lights. So on the 1952 models (in practice, about a month before 1951-season production ended), they were relocated on the noses of the front wings.

The "bulkhead" sidelamps were Lucas 451 units with frosted lenses and chromed rims, and the "wing" sidelamps were Lucas 52139 units. All bulbs had a 6-watt rating, and a Lucas no 207 type was used in the "bulkhead" lights while a Lucas no 989 was used in the later type. The "wing" sidelamps had a chromed surround to the lens, which was held in place by a bead on the rubber mounting base and had to be levered away from the bead when a bulb was changed. For a list of the chassis numbers at which the "wing" sidelights were introduced, see the section on Bulkheads above.

The 80-inch Land Rovers exported to the USA always had sidelights mounted in the front wings. In this case, they were Lucas 488 units, and the positions for the bulkhead-mounted lamps were blanked off with a circular metal plate. By contrast, early models exported to Canada did retain the standard bulkhead-mounted lamps.

Tail lights

All 80-inch Land Rovers except those for the USA had Lucas D-shaped tail lamps with a black body, type ST51/1. These contained a 21-watt bulb for the brake light and a 5-watt bulb for the tail light. The 5-watt bulb was also used to illuminate the rear number-plate on the side where this was mounted, through a clear glass section on the underside of the lamp. On the other side, a metal blanking plate that was painted to match the lamp

The 80-inch models exported to North America had a central rear number-plate with its own fixing bracket and lamp. Early ones certainly had a black body; later ones may have had a chrome finish.

body replaced the clear lens.

The 80-inch Land Rovers exported to the USA had Lucas 488 round tail lights that contained double-filament bulbs for the tail and stop functions. They were let into the tail panels and a cover plate was riveted over the pre-drilled fixing holes for the standard D-lamps. US regulations also required that the rear number-plate should be mounted centrally, so a Lucas 53093E lamp with a black body was added to the number-plate mounting on 1951 models, and a Lucas 53101E/J on 1952-1953 models.

Lighting regulations differ around the world and are occasionally updated, which can present problems for restorers. In Britain, the 1953 Transport Lighting Act that became effective from 1 October 1954 introduced new requirements. It meant that all existing and new vehicles had to display two red reflectors at the rear; and of course none of the 80-inch models had ever had any. So Rover's Spares Department provided some. These were round items with a chromed frame and were to be fitted by drilling a hole 2 1/16in (52mm) in from the body side and 25/32in (20mm) from the bottom of each tail panel, and using the single-screw fixing provided. Some owners went with the factory recommendation; others used proprietary reflectors of various sizes.

Two years after that, British regulations changed to require all vehicles registered before 1 October 1954 to carry two rear lamps (many older cars had only one), each with an illuminated diameter of 2 inches. Rover advised their dealers in a Service Bulletin dated October 1956 that the D-lamps on the 80-inch Land Rover did not comply with this latter requirement. They suggested a simple change to Lucas number 53390 lamps that did meet the new regulations, which came into effect on 1 October 1956. These were again D-shaped lamps, but did not have the separate rectangular lens strip of the original type. Once again, some owners followed the factory recommendation and others did not, which explains why so many early Land Rovers in Britain have been fitted with non-original tail lamps.

Direction indicators

As explained above, direction indicators were not fitted as standard equipment to any 80-inch Land Rovers. The custom in Britain when these vehicles were new was still to use hand signals to indicate an intention to turn. Optional semaphore-arm "trafficators" were available, and are described in the chapter on Optional Equipment.

Direction indicator lights are a legal requirement in most countries today, and enthusiasts have found multiple (and sometimes ingenious) ways of fitting such lights unobtrusively to early Land Rovers. For those who prefer not to drill the body panels to fit additional lights, it is usually possible to find a way of fitting them on brackets. Before embarking on such an installation, it is important to be absolutely certain about the legal requirements in the country where the vehicle is to be used.

ELECTRICAL ITEMS

The towing plug was mounted in the rear cross-member and was protected by a black rubber plug when not in use. Two of the four fixing screws on this one can be seen.

With the cover removed, the towing plug looked like this.

Early towing plugs had no protective cover on the inner side of the rear cross-member.

This is the way the towing plug was attached to the cross-member on an early chassis, R86-0027. Note the protective cover where the wiring enters the chassis rail. The exhaust hanger bracket is also clear here.

Towing plug

After October 1948, all 80-inch models came as standard with a pre-wired towing plug, which was recessed into the right-hand side of the rear cross-member. The three pin connections were an earth at the top, a feed to the stop lamp at bottom left, and a feed to the tail lamp at bottom right. These three-pin plugs no longer meet road traffic requirements in some countries.

There were some small changes to the plug's mounting arrangements during 1949. At 866-6068 in May that year, the L-shaped plate connecting the plug to the chassis was replaced by a C-shaped plate with four bolt holes, and the rear cross-member was drilled around the trailer plug hole to receive the four bolts. There was no splash cover for the plug at this stage, but a month or so later, at 866-7200, Rover standardised a black rubber cover with a short brass chain that retained it to the rim around the plug. This arrangement then lasted until the end of 80-inch production in 1953.

INTERIOR & TOOLS

This section looks at the interior of the cab or driving compartment, including the seats, instruments, controls, tool kit and vehicle handbook. The interior of the body tub is covered in the earlier section on Bodywork.

There were several optional items available. The heater, engine governor controls, and direction indicator (trafficator) controls are all covered in the chapter about Optional Equipment.

Instrument panel

All the 80-inch models had the same type of instrument panel, which was lozenge-shaped and was mounted in the centre of the dashboard to suit both right-hand drive and left-hand drive. The panel itself was pressed from steel and was held by four set screws and washers to a pod welded to the bulkhead. The front surface of the panel was always painted in the body colour.

The instrument panel on all 80s had the same lozenge shape. This is it on a carefully restored August 1949 model.

INTERIOR & TOOLS

The instrument panel was not handed to suit left-hand or right-hand drive. Reading from left to right, its main items were a combined ignition and lighting switch, an ammeter, a fuel gauge and a speedometer. These were interspersed with warning lights, a switch and a two-pin power socket.

Instruments and switches

The combined ignition and lighting switch had a rotary switch and a key-operated barrel lock in its centre. The switch was a Lucas PLC6 L133 type, and the face of the barrel lock was very helpfully stamped with the number of the ignition key – ideal both for replacing lost keys and creating unauthorised ones!

The ammeter had its scale at the top of the gauge and its needle pointed upwards. On the 1.6-litre models, this was a Lucas CZ26 L8 (part no 364595) with a red-tipped needle and a scale reading from -20 amps to +20amps. It was then changed, probably at the start of 2-litre production, to one with a white-tipped needle and a scale reading from -30 to +30amps. This later type was a Lucas CZU26 L3, with part number 36047.

The fuel gauge had a larger diameter than the ammeter and its needle pointed downwards to the scale at the bottom of the gauge. This was not manufactured by Lucas but by Jaeger. The same gauge was used on all 80-inch models.

The largest dial was the speedometer on the extreme right. This was another Jaeger instrument and was marked up to 70mph (although the scale actually went to 77mph). It incorporated a distance recorder. Either miles-per-hour or kilometres-per-hour types could be fitted, to suit the intended destination. A second type of speedometer was fitted when the axle ratio changed in approximately September 1948, and the two types of speedometer are distinguished by markings on their faces: the early one for the 4.88:1 axle ratio shows 1575 revolutions per mile, and the one for the later 4.7:1 ratio shows 1500 revolutions per mile.

The only other switch on the panel was for the instrument lighting, and was a push-pull type mounted at the upper left. It was a Lucas PS15/1 L4 type with an unpainted metal bezel and a black Bakelite knob. The knob tended to crack at its threaded end, and when supplies of the original pattern were used up it appears that Rover provided a Service replacement with a clear plastic body and a black top. Below this switch were sockets for an inspection lamp, with plastic colour-coded surrounds in black (above, for the earth pin) and red (below, for the live pin). These were Lucas units, listed under part number 301187.

Warning lights

There were normally three warning lights, for ignition, oil pressure and choke. Two were located between the ignition-and-lighting switch and the ammeter. The upper one had an amber lens and was for the choke (or mixture control) and the lower one had a red lens and was for the ignition and low charge warning. The third warning light was between the ammeter and the fuel gauge, level with the ignition light, and this

Ready to receive the front plate with its instruments, this is the instrument housing on a 1953 2-litre model.

The early speedometer used with the 4.88:1 axles was marked just above the needle with the figure 1575, for revolutions per mile….

… and the later and more common one, for the 4.7:1 axles, was marked with the figure of 1500.

The Cold Start control is seen here on a 1948 model, R86-1164. Note the position of the hooked hand throttle control to its left.....

... while on this 1953-model fire engine the hand throttle is on the right of the Cold Start control. The ribbed black button in the centre below the instrument panel is the starter button.

was a red one for the oil pressure.

There were also three types of warning light, the first type used on 1.6-litre models up to the middle of the 1951 model-year, the second type on the late 1.6-litres and on early 2-litres, and the third from late in the 1952 season until the end of 80-inch production.

The first type had a metal body and bezel and a plastic lens; some lenses were flat, others were domed. The oil warning light had a disc inserted behind its red lens with the word OIL punched out of it. The second type were Lucas WL3/1 units with lens and bezel moulded as a single plastic part; there was no lettering for the green oil warning light. These were introduced in January 1951 at chassis numbers 1610-1656, 1613-3214, 1616-1502, 1630-0004, 1633-0004, 1636-0008, 1663-0043 and 1666-1477.

The third type was again made of plastic, but this time with a separate glass lens. These had black bezels and were introduced in early April 1952 at chassis numbers 2610-5067, 2613-3551, 2616-2760, 2663-0362 and 2666-0967. The red ignition light was a Lucas 38084A, the green oil light was a Lucas 38085A, and the amber choke light was a Lucas 38086A.

80-inch models destined for the USA had an additional warning light for the headlamp main beam, and this was of a different type and had a blue lens. It was mounted in the instrument panel above the oil pressure warning light. Some examples have been found on non-US models built in the 1949 season, and it is possible that these were overstocks that were used to meet a shortfall of the standard instrument panels on the production lines.

All warning lights had 2.5-watt bulbs, but the bulb holders differ between those with metal bodies and those with plastic bodies. There were two types of speedometer cable, the earlier one with a ribbed outer casing and the later one with a plain outer casing. The first type was used up to chassis number 0610-5830.

There were also several optional instruments, which are covered in the chapter on Optional Equipment.

Bulkhead controls

Additional controls were fitted elsewhere on the bulkhead, and there were three of them: starter button, hand throttle, and choke.

The starter button was always under the left-hand side of the instrument panel, and had the same black-finished alloy knob on all 80-inch models. (The ignition key did not also operate the starter, as on more modern vehicles.) Below the right of the instrument panel was a curved metal handle with a sherardised finish, which could be used to adjust the idling speed when the vehicle was stationary. Rover called this the hand throttle control, but it had a much more limited range of operation than the optional Engine Governor (see the Optional Equipment chapter), whose control quadrant would also be mounted to the bulkhead below the instrument panel.

The choke control was located towards the right of the instrument panel and below it, in the form of a black plastic knob bearing the legend "Cold Start" in white. This was mounted on a steel bracket that was bolted to the bulkhead, and there were two variants of this bracket. The first type was in two parts, bolted together. The second type was essentially the same but was a single-piece assembly, and was introduced at chassis number 0610-4683 in November 1949. From late April 1950 and chassis number 0611-1528, the choke knob and cable assembly was modified so that it could be bolted directly to the bulkhead without a supporting bracket.

The choke cable always operated a Lucas S4C switch that was bolted to the bulkhead-mounted bracket and operated the choke warning light. Note that this was not designed to illuminate only when the engine had reached working temperature as a warning to put the choke in; it simply indicated that the choke was in use.

This plate alongside the instrument panel offered guidance on use of the transfer box selector control.

On later models, the transfer box instruction plate also displayed the chassis number. This is it on a 1953 2-litre model, 3610-2343.

Major controls

The major controls consisted of the steering wheel, gear and transfer box levers, freewheel control, handbrake and pedals.

Steering wheel and column

The steering wheel always had a black plastic rim over a metal armature, with a chrome finish for its spokes. The black Bakelite centre boss contained a switch of the same material that controlled the headlight dipping system. Moulded into the boss alongside the switch was the word DIP, with an arrow pointing left, and both word and arrow were painted white.

The steering wheel on the first 300-400 Land Rovers up to about October 1948 was a Rover car type, with three pairs of two spokes. There were thick walls for the hub and the car-type indicator ring was retained. This was replaced by a similar design from a different supplier that had three pairs of four spokes for additional strength and was specific to Land Rovers.

The first few hundred Land Rovers had a two-spoke Rover car steering wheel.

This general view of the driving area of an August 1949 model shows that the two-spoke steering wheel was back again after a few months' absence. Clearly visible are the unique accelerator pedal design and the red-knobbed transfer box control lever. The dull finish of all the bolt heads and washers is correct.

However, this second type gave trouble because of poor quality Bakelite.

So as a third stage, the two-spoke Rover car wheel was used again from late in the 1949 season, its introduction roughly coinciding with the standardisation of Bronze Green paint. This was clearly a temporary measure, however, and early in the 1950 season the definitive steering wheel made its appearance. This one had three sets of four spokes, no indicator ring, and a hub with thinner walls. It was also slightly dished where the earlier wheels had been flat.

The steering column was always painted black and was supported by a bracket that was bolted to the cab side of the bulkhead. Both the bracket and the clamp that held the column to it were galvanised.

There was a change in March 1953 to the inner steering column, which until that point had a bronze nut at its lower end. It was replaced by a case-hardened inner column with a steel nut, at chassis numbers 3610-3433, 3613-3245, 3616-2792, 3663-3498 and 3666-1341.

INTERIOR & TOOLS

Gear lever (main)

The main gear lever was always cranked to suit left-hand or right-hand steering positions as appropriate, for this reason the LHD and RHD types are not interchangeable. All gear levers were painted black. There were two different types but both had the same black plastic grip, which had the gate positions marked on it in white characters.

The earlier type of gear lever was used only on the first 1500 vehicles, and was mounted to the gearbox cover. All subsequent vehicles had a different type that was mounted to the gearbox itself. There was a further minor change to the gear lever during 1953 production, at gearbox number 3610-2305.

The gear lever grommet on all early models was a flat type attached to the gearbox cover by eight bifurcated rivets. In late August 1949 from chassis number 0610-1033, the gearbox cover was no longer pre-drilled to take the rivets and the gear lever grommet changed to a push-fit type that simplified assembly.

Transfer box controls

The levers for the transfer box evolved along with the transmission design, and went through three stages. In all cases, the shafts of the levers were painted black.

On all models, the transfer box was operated by a lever with a red knob, mounted on the right-hand side of the gearbox cover. Pushing the lever forwards selected High range for road work; pulling the lever back to its mid-position transferred the drive to the Power Take-Off and represented a neutral position; pulling the lever back to its rearmost position selected Low range for off-road driving.

Up to early November 1949, the freewheel was locked by a ring-pull control in the floor on the driver's side, which was attached by a cable to the operating lever. This worked only when the transfer box was in Low ratio, and the freewheel was automatically unlocked for normal use when High ratio was engaged. This control did not change sides to suit the position of the steering wheel, which made it less than readily accessible to the driver of a left-hand-drive vehicle. Beginning

A second view of the August 1949 model gives a clearer view of the handbrake lever with its unpainted press-button, and of the floor-mounted ring-pull control for the freewheel.

FACTORY-ORIGINAL LAND ROVER SERIES I, 80-INCH MODELS

An examination of the cab area of this vehicle shows a three-spoke steering wheel and a yellow knob for the freewheel control lever; on the dashboard, the red instruction label for use of the freewheel has faded, but is still clear.

at chassis number 0610-3885, the ring-pull was replaced by a lever control, mounted more accessibly to the right of the main gearlever and distinguished by a yellow knob. There was also a spring on the shaft of this control, and the lever had to be pushed down against it to lock the freewheel.

On the 1951 and later models, which had selectable four-wheel drive (and no freewheel), the lever with the yellow knob could be pushed down to disengage drive to the front axle. This control again had a spring on its shaft that automatically returned it to the "normal" position for four-wheel drive when Low range was engaged.

As a reminder of the workings of the transmission, Rover fitted a metal plate to the bulkhead with an explanation. On all vehicles fitted with a freewheel, this plate was printed in red. On later vehicles with the selectable system, the plate was printed in black and had an explanatory diagram as well. These later plates also had the chassis number stamped into them.

Handbrake

The pull-up handbrake was always mounted through the heel-board, on the side appropriate to the position of the steering wheel and pedals. There were different types for right-hand-drive and left-hand drive models, and there were two different basic shapes of handbrake as well. All handbrakes were painted black and had an unpainted press-button release in the end. There is evidence suggesting that some vehicles were fitted on assembly with the handbrake from the Rover P3 saloon car, with a longer handle that was also chromed; this presumably happened when there were shortages on the line.

The earlier type of handbrake had a Bakelite grip over the end of its shaft, while the later type had a simple straight metal shaft. The release button was also smaller on the later type. The change was made in December 1949, and the later handbrake was first fitted at chassis number 0610-5379. It did not reach left-hand drive models until early May 1950, at chassis number 0611-1807.

The right-hand-drive and left-hand-drive versions of these two handbrakes are not interchangeable, because the left-hand-drive versions are welded to a cross-shaft that has no counterpart on right-hand-drive models.

Pedals

The accelerator was a pendant type, with a distinctively shaped pedal that pivoted from the toe-board. From mid-April 1951, the pedal shaft was lengthened to accommodate a distance piece, but there were differences between the RHD and LHD installations. The changes took place at chassis numbered 1610-2849, 1613-4922, 1616-2141, 1630-0004, 1633-0007, 1636-0009, 1663-0079 and 1666-1897.

Both the clutch pedal and the brake pedal acted on rods that passed through the floor panel to cross-shafts underneath. Both pedals had a series of raised "pips" to give grip, and one side of each pedal was also turned up for the same reason; this was the right-hand side of the clutch pedal and the left-hand side of the brake, the two raised sections being adjacent when installed to prevent a muddy workboot from sliding off one pedal and onto the next. Each pedal rod had a rubber dust-seal where it passed through the floor panel.

Seats and interior

At the start of 80-inch production in summer 1948, Land Rovers were provided with only a driver's seat as standard; the centre and passenger seats were extra-cost options. How many were actually sold with just the one seat is simply not known, but by October that year Rover had decided to make the two additional seats part of the standard specification. Three seats were then fitted to all 80-inch models as standard, except when a Centre PTO was fitted. In such cases, no centre seat was fitted, to allow access to the controls for the PTO.

Inward-facing seats could be fitted in the back body, but these were always an optional extra and are therefore covered here in the chapter about Optional Equipment. Note that there was no rear-view mirror as standard on the windscreen header rail; the round mirror mounted to the driver's side windscreen pillar was considered sufficient for a commercial vehicle at the time. Most owners today have fitted a conventional rear-view mirror for additional safety; in Britain, new regulations introduced in January 1958 required dual-purpose vehicles (such as Land Rovers) to have an external mirror on the driver's side and either a second external mirror on the passenger's side or an internal mirror.

Four distinct types of "cab" seat were used during 80-inch production. Good-quality reproductions of all of them have been made available.

The very simple seat design pioneered on the pre-production models was carried over to the first 150 or so production vehicles. The curved bar-type backrests were unchanged but the production design of cushion was improved with a wedge shape that gave some under-thigh support. Green Vynide trim

The earliest models had crude seat backs with no more than a curved cushion to provide support. These views show the internal structure of such a seat back, and one with the cushion in place (seen here on pre-production model R14).

was standard, but it is not impossible that some black-trimmed items left over from pre-production assembly were also used up as production got under way.

The cushions were built up around a simple wooden frame that was padded and covered with Vynide that was attached by screws and cup washers underneath. There was a cylindrical locating rubber screwed in place mid-way along each side section, and these rubbers located in holes in the seatbox to hold the cushion in place. The rest of the underside of each cushion was covered in hessian with a natural brown finish.

The second type of seat design, introduced in October 1948 at approximately chassis number 86-1501, is known as the "spade" type because of the shape of the backrest, which tapers towards the top. Each backrest was bolted to a sprung loop that was in turn bolted to the capping on the forward edge of the body tub. These loops used different fixing holes from the earlier backrests, and the drillings for the earlier type remained

These are the spade-type seat backs on an August 1949 model. The wedge shape of the cushions is clearly visible.

The spade-type seat backs were sprung against the capping on the front edge of the body tub.

in the body cappings for some time after the change to the spade-type seats was made. Each backrest also had a rubber buffer that was attached by screw and nut.

These spade-type backrests were built up around an aluminium alloy panel that was then lightly padded and trimmed with green Vynide. As before, the seat cushions were wedge-shaped and had rubber locating blocks screwed to their undersides.

The third type of seat is known as the "shovel back" type, again on account of its shape. This was introduced in early April 1950, theoretically at chassis 0611-0305. This type of seat had a hinged back that could be folded forwards to allow long loads carried in the back body to project over the passenger seats. The accompanying cushion was noticeably deeper than before.

These shovel-type seat backs were built up around a steel

The final type of seat back is seen here in a 1953 fire engine, where the upholstery was in red rather than the standard green.

inner panel, again lightly padded and trimmed in green Vynide. Two long sherardised hinges were bolted to each seat back, and their lower ends were bolted through a cross-piece that was in turn bolted to the front of the body tub. When upright, each seatback was held in place by a webbing strap that was riveted to one of the hinges and had an eyelet at the other end. The eyelets went over studs attached to the top surface of the body capping behind the seat. Some of these studs incorporated distance pieces. There was also a rubber buffer block on the back of each hinge, held in place by screws and rivets, which prevented the seatback from touching the body capping. These blocks were hollow extrusions, the cavities providing a degree of springing to cushion the seatback against shocks transmitted through the body.

After about 6000 vehicles had been built during the 1952 season, the fourth and final type of seat became standard. The actual changeover points were recorded as chassis numbers 2610-2281, 2613-1714, 2616-1500, 2630-0003, 2633-0008, 2636-0002, 2663-0151 and 2666-0355. Cushions remained unchanged, but the seat backs became squarer and flatter, with more padding than before. Green Vynide covering was again standard. These seats were mounted on pivots rather than hinges; the pivots were at the bottom corner of each backrest and depended on brackets that were held to the seat base by screws and nuts. There was a single bracket at each outside edge of the seat, and a double bracket between each outer seat and the centre seat. There was a leather retaining strap on the left rear of each seatback, and a leather buffer pad on the right. Retaining straps did the same job as before, and their eyelets went over studs held to the body capping by drive screws. There were also two rubber buffer blocks on the body capping for each seat, secured by drive screws.

> **INTERIOR COLOURS & TRIMS**
>
> The only "trim" as conventionally understood was on the seats of an 80-inch Land Rover. This was dark green Vynide as standard, although it is possible that there were minor variations in the colour over the years.
>
> Red seats were standard on Fire Engines from June 1952, and it is possible that other colours were supplied to special order, but these would have been very rare.

Tool kit

All 80-inch models were supplied with wheel-changing tools, a tyre pump, and a set of hand tools in a black hessian roll. A starting handle was an extra-cost option on the very first models but was made standard in October 1948.

The wheel-changing tools consisted of a wheelbrace and a jack. The wheelbrace was a double-cranked type and was always painted black. The screw jack was made by Shelley and came with a separate extension bar and removable handle. The jack and extension bar were normally black, and the handle was either unpainted or sometimes black. The extension bar could be stowed in a pair of clips on the left-hand side panel of the back body, but the handle, the jack itself and the wheelbrace were normally kept in the stowage locker in the seatbox.

Also supplied with each vehicle was a hand-operated tyre pump (with connecting hose), which was usually painted black. Export models came with a tyre lever, but this was not standard in Britain. Pump and lever were both normally kept in the locker in the passenger's side of the seatbox locker. The starting handle was normally painted black and had its own dedicated stowage clips on the front panel of the body tub.

The hand tools came in a black hessian roll with two string ties, and this would also have been stowed in the seatbox locker. A full set of 12 tools in an original roll is a rare find today.

It is important to note that there were variations in the tools supplied over the years, probably caused by supply shortages, so the list shown below should be considered as representing a typical complement and not as definitive. The tools themselves were mostly the same as those supplied with Rover cars of the time, although for the cars they were fitted into a rubber-lined tray. The screwdriver was also simpler than the one supplied for the cars, which had a wooden handle.

Vehicle handbook

All 80-inch models came with a vehicle handbook, more properly known as the Land Rover Operation Manual. This was initially stowed loose in the seatbox locker, but when stiffeners were added under the locker lid, these doubled as a holder for the handbook.

The early handbook had a green and beige cover, with a drawing of a Land Rover. There were several editions, each one carrying its identification number and publication date on the first page. These were TP/108/A (June 1948), TP/108/B (October 1948), TP/108/C (August 1949) and TP/108/D (April 1950); the April 1950 issue claimed to cover all models from 1948 to 1951.

Of interest is that there was a matching Repair Charges book, dating from September 1949 and numbered TP/120/A.

From the start of the 1951 season in October 1950, handbooks carried two identifying numbers. One was a four-digit part number and the other was the publication number. Although the publication number suffix letter changed with each revision of the handbook, the part number remained the same. These had a different cover, which was all green.

The part number for the UK editions of these later manuals was 3909, and there were five known editions. These were TP/131/A (October 1950), TP/131/B, TP/131/C (July 1951), TP/131/D (November 1951), and TP/131/E (May 1952).

There were also some foreign-language versions of the TP/131 series handbooks. The known ones have parts numbers 3907 and 3910 (both French), 3916 and 3916A (Spanish), and 3948 (Portuguese).

Note that Land Rover did not publish a handbook in German. There was, however, a special German handbook published for the 80-inch Tempo models (see the final chapter) that were built for the West German Bundesgrenzschutz. This was dated April 1953.

> **TOOL KIT**
>
> The list is as follows:
>
> | | |
> |---|---|
> | Grease gun | brass body |
> | Tyre pressure gauge | with Rover crest cast into its body |
> | Tommy bar | |
> | Box spanner | |
> | 7in spark plug wrench | |
> | Combination pliers | |
> | Screwdriver | with loop-type steel handle |
> | Distributor screwdriver | manufactured by Lucas |
> | Feeler gauge | manufactured by Lucas |
> | Adjustable spanner | manufactured by King Dick |
> | Double-ended spanner | 3/16in and ¼in AF |
> | Double-ended spanner | 5/16in and 7/16in |
> | Single-ended spanner | 3/8in AF |

The early handbooks – Operation Manuals to Rover – had this design of cover.

THE TICKFORD STATION WAGONS

Now part of the historic vehicle fleet belonging to JLR Classic, this Station Wagon was first registered in November 1949. It was superbly restored by the late Ken Wheelwright, and shows the optional two-tone finish with Light Green on the upper panels and Bronze Green below.

Rover announced the Land Rover Station Wagon at the Commercial Motor Show in October 1948, displaying a prototype vehicle on the company stand. Availability theoretically began in December 1948, but in practice production did not begin until May 1949.

The basic shape and configuration of the Station Wagon probably originated with Rover, but the design was refined and put into production by Tickford Ltd, of Newport Pagnell, who under their earlier identity of Salmons & Sons had built drophead coupé bodies for Rover cars in the 1930s. Tickford built the bodies in the traditional coachbuilder's style, with aluminium alloy panels over a wooden frame, which added considerably to the manufacturing cost.

British car production was necessarily still biased towards production for export, and almost all the 1949 models were shipped abroad. There was some production for the home market during the 1950 season, but sales were slow. The main reason was cost: the basic cost of a Tickford Station Wagon was around 50% more than that of a standard Land Rover and, because it was a passenger-carrying vehicle, it was

FACTORY-ORIGINAL LAND ROVER SERIES I, 80-INCH MODELS

This very late model – the second to last made – shows the more common single-colour paintwork and the later style of tailgate with concealed pivots in place of four hinges.

also subject to Purchase Tax. This put the showroom price up to the same level as that of a quality saloon car, As a result, most of the 480 Station Wagons built as 1950 models went for export.

The company had clearly decided to discontinue the model before the end of the 1950 season, but did build a final batch of 100 examples, mostly to meet outstanding export orders. These were sold as 1951 models, but all their chassis had probably been completed before October 1950.

There were 650 examples of the production Tickford Station Wagon, plus one pre-production prototype. Like all coachbuilt bodies built by hand over a period of time, the Tickford bodies were subject to minor variations of detail. The notes in this chapter should therefore be considered as generally descriptive rather than prescriptive for a restoration.

CHASSIS AND SUSPENSION

The Tickford Station Wagon was built on a standard 80-inch chassis of the time, and in that respect its development followed that of the standard models. Most Station Wagon chassis had the Dark Green paint that became standard in summer 1949, although the coachbuilder's prototype (built on pre-production model L.20) had a galvanised chassis and a small number of early production models had Light Green chassis.

The Station Wagon body was longer than the standard type and overhung the rear of the chassis by a few inches. This overhang was supported by small box-like extensions on the rear cross-member, a modification that was almost certainly carried out by Tickford and not on the Rover assembly lines.

The earliest models had fishplate brackets welded to the

front dumb-irons to take the standard front bumper, but during the 1950 season (at chassis number 0620-0091), the dumb-irons were drilled to take bolts and the attachment brackets were welded to the front bumper instead.

The first Station Wagons were supplied with standard road springs, but the 1950 and 1951 models had the heavy-duty rear springs that were also specified for the Welder and Compressor models. The switch to 2½in front springs with shackles at the rear was made at chassis number 0620-0420. Early models had 1T8-C4 dampers all round up to chassis number 0620-0409, when the rear dampers changed to the 4T8-A6 type.

WHEELS

Wheels were always the same as those on contemporary standard 80-inch Land Rovers. They were normally painted to match the bodywork or, on two-tone Station Wagons, to match the darker colour.

ENGINE, TRANSMISSION AND EXHAUST

All the engines in the Tickford Station Wagons were 1.6-litre types; the model went out of production around a year before the 2-litre engine was introduced. There were no differences from the 1.6-litre engines in the standard Land Rovers of the time.

All details of the transmission were also exactly the same as those on contemporary standard 80-inch models. All Station Wagons had a freewheel in the transmission, operated by a ring-pull in the right-hand front floor up to late 1949 and by a lever with a yellow grip thereafter. Although the last 100 Station Wagons were nominally built to the 1951-season specification, their chassis were assembled before the changeover to a selectable four-wheel-drive transmission in October 1950.

Right-hand-drive models up to and including 0620-0286 had the early type of exhaust tailpipe mounting described earlier in the book, and this mounting changed in the same way as on the basic Land Rover models.

BODY

All panels forward of the bulkhead were exactly the same as those on the contemporary standard Land Rover. For the Station Wagons, the change from the full grille to the "lights-through" type came in May 1950, and chassis number 0620-0311 was theoretically the first with the new style.

The bonnet came as standard with the spare wheel mounting that was an optional extra on other models, and this was accompanied by a unique cover spun from light alloy. The cover was attached to its central support rod by a large butterfly nut. Only one size of cover was supplied, although in theory the Station Wagon could be ordered with either standard 6.00x16 or wider 7.00x16 size tyres.

Everything was different from standard from the bulkhead to the back of the body. The Station Wagon body was assembled by traditional coachbuilding methods, using hand-beaten panels over a wooden frame that was made and assembled by hand. The outer or "skin" panels were made from the same Birmabright BB2 as the standard Land Rover body, and the wooden frame was bolted together and was reinforced with metal flitch plates. The panels were attached to the frame with coachbuilder's nails, and many of the fixings were by coachbolts rather than the screws, set screws and bolts used in the standard Land Rover.

Body frame

There are differing opinions about the type of wood used in the frame. Coachbuilders had traditionally used seasoned ash, but there were two reasons why this was not used for the Land Rover Station Wagon. One was that it was in short supply in the immediate post-war years (the ash wood had not been laid down to "season" in wartime), and the other was that it was not best suited to conditions in many of the export markets where Rover hoped to sell the vehicles. Dennis Mynard, writing in *Salmons & Sons, the Tickford Coachbuilders*, described it as rosa peroba, a dense hardwood that was grown in south-eastern Brazil and was termite-proof. John Smith, in *Land Rover, the Formative Years*, believed it was Iroko wood, a tropical hardwood that will not rot in tropical climates.

The wooden body frame consisted of a front "hoop" attached to the bulkhead; a bracing panel running across the bulkhead at the top; two side frames with forward extensions over the door apertures that met the front frame at the

The last examples of the Tickford Station Wagon had the "lights-through" front end associated with the 1951 models.

The Tickford Station Wagons depended on a traditional wooden body frame, to which the outer skin panels were attached by coachbuilder's nails.

The wooden body structure is vulnerable to severe deterioration over time. This is one of the front pillars.

This view shows the wooden frame outboard of the bulkhead, and the way the door skins wrapped over their own wooden frames. The vehicle is a very original Tickford that survives in Nairobi with under 45,000 miles on the clock. (Christopher Race)

windscreen header rail; a straight beam across the rear at roof level; and three wooden roof bearers. The frames of the doors and tailgate sections were also wooden.

Body panels

Although Rover dutifully gave every section a part number, it is highly unlikely that any of these parts were ever kept in the Rover Service department. As these bodies were hand-built, there was plenty of scope for dimensional variations, and all panels would have been "fitted" in the traditional way at Tickford. Any demand for replacement of body panels would almost certainly have been referred straight to Tickford, who would then create what was needed as a bespoke part.

The outer skin panels for the doors and side panels incorporated three swage lines. It is possible that these were a conscious echo of the design used on the Jeep Station Wagon (a much larger vehicle on a 104-inch wheelbase); the idea there was to simulate the wooden battens of a traditional American "woodie" body. Equally likely is the possibility that the swages were a design feature introduced by Tickford, perhaps both to add strength to the panels and to reduce drumming. They unquestionably added visual interest to what would otherwise have been a very plain-looking design.

Bulkhead

The standard Land Rover bulkhead was retained but was modified considerably. Tickford bolted the wooden uprights of

THE TICKFORD STATION WAGONS

A feature unique to the Tickford is the spun alloy wheel cover, which is secured by a large wing nut.

the front body frame to its sides, with the result that the Station Wagon body was wider than the standard Land Rover type, and had a noticeable "step" between front wing and body on each side.

In addition, the bulkhead was modified by an extension that ran across its top face and provided an open oddments box on each side. This extension was attached to the wooden bracing panel between the front pillars by woodscrews. Each oddments box was lined, probably with black felt over a cardboard stiffener, and there was a metal plate between each end of the extension panel and the body pillar. The whole assembly was painted in the main body colour, to match the bulkhead itself.

Seatbox and front floor

The whole of the seatbox and front floor area was different from its equivalent on the standard 80-inch Land Rover. The seatbox assembly covered only two-thirds of the body width, leaving a flat floor area on the left-hand side where a tipping seat could be mounted. This arrangement was the same on both left-hand-drive and right-hand-drive models, because the raised seatbox was necessary to clear the fuel tank which remained in the same place on the right-hand side regardless of the steering position.

The seatbox had a flap with a piano hinge to give access to the tank filler, and a second, smaller flap to cover the access hole for the Centre PTO. (Whether any Station Wagons were

The sliding windows in the rear of the body have metal finger grips on the inside. This one has a reinforced metal edge that was not standard and may not be original.

107

actually equipped with PTOs is of course rather doubtful.) These flaps were similar but not identical to their equivalents on the standard Land Rover.

The floor section consisted of a main panel with an extension panel in the toebox area, and the assembly was reinforced by a strengthening channel at the side, a vertical rear panel and a shaped section described as a chassis cover panel. Riveted to the back of the floor section was a seat stop against which the tubular frame of the tipping seat rested.

Forming the rear of the seatbox, and acting as a stiffener for the rear floor assembly, was a two piece vertical panel. Its two sections were bolted together, and the whole assembly was bolted to the seatbox at the top and the rear floor at the bottom. On the rear face of this were riveted two small tool clips and three medium-sized ones, and these were used for stowage of the wheelbrace and jack handle.

Doors

The two side doors were full-height types that incorporated drop-glasses and quarter-lights. They were each hung on two partly concealed hinges, attached between the leading edge of the wooden door frame and the wooden bulkhead extension pillar. There was a simple car-type handle at waist height on each one, and the handle on the driver's side incorporated a keylock.

The metal window frames and channels were inserted into the door and bolted in place. The mechanisms for the drop-glasses were also mounted to the wooden door frames. They were operated by cables from the handle on the inside of the door (see below); the original cable was a Teleflex type.

There were chromed metal frames for the opening quarter-lights, which pivoted centrally on pins that passed into the upper and lower window frames. The windows themselves were made of glass, and the lower part of each chromed frame had a catch that engaged with the main window frame to hold the quarter-light closed. Unusually, these catches were cast from bronze and remained unpainted.

The door skin panels were far more complex than they appear, with capping plates at the top, bottom and sides in addition to the main panel that ran from top to bottom and embraced the window frame as well. The main panel incorporated three horizontal swages that lined up with similar swages in the body sides.

Tailboard and rear window

The Station Wagon body had what would nowadays be called a horizontally-split tailgate, with a top-hinged window and a drop-down tailboard. Both were unique to the vehicle. There were two types of drop-down tailboard.

Both versions of the drop-down lower tailboard had a wooden inner frame and an outer panel of Birmabright BB2, into which was pressed an image of part of the wooden framework underneath. There were actually five wooden

The tailgate chains were sheathed in green vinyl to match the interior trim.

uprights, but only four were shown on the outer skin panel. The inside surface of this tailboard was fully panelled, and was painted in the body colour (probably always the darker one if there were two). The panel was held in place by unpainted rubbing strips that were screwed through it to the wooden frame underneath. The whole tailboard was supported when open by a chain on each side, attached to hooks on the tailboard itself and to retaining brackets bolted to the rear body frame.

A catch on each side of the lower tailboard engaged with a receiver on the rear frame to hold the tailboard closed. The catches were disengaged by turning a handle that acted on rods connected to them; the handle was mounted near the top of the tailboard and held to the wooden frame by woodscrews. It was a proprietary T-shaped type with a chromed finish. The Land Rover badge was mounted to the top right of the tailboard, and the number-plate was mounted centrally with a

THE TICKFORD STATION WAGONS

An early left-hand-drive model (L867-0031) was evaluated by the Army at Chertsey. This picture shows the early type of tailgate with four external hinges, and also gives a clear view of the two-tone colour option. The rear lighting arrangements here are also original, with just one red lamp mounted below the tailboard on each side.

The later pattern tailgate had a cleaner appearance than the original, without the external hinges.

The later pattern of tailgate had a single large pivot bolt on each side.

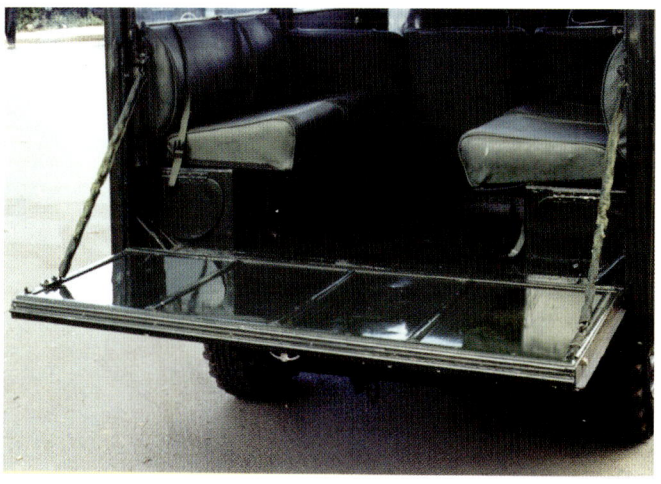

Inside surfaces of the early and late tailgates compared. The early one has "framed" edges (and in this case the three rubbing-strips are painted). The later one has plain edges and (again in this case) unpainted rubbing strips.

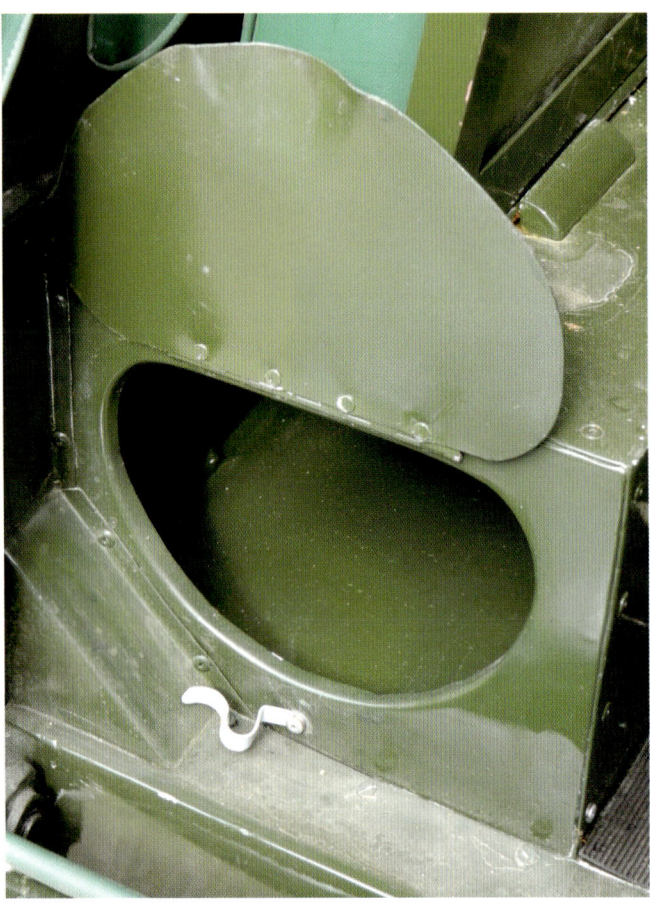

Hinged lids give access to the lockers behind the rear wheels. Note the unpainted metal spring clip designed to hold this one closed.

The upper tailgate has a spring-loaded arm on each side that can be locked to hold it open.

special mounting bracket. This bracket was similar in concept to the one used for the number-plate on standard 80-inch models shipped to the USA (see the section on the standard Tailboard, earlier), but was not hinged. For the rear lighting arrangements, please see the section on Lighting, below.

The lower tailboard was modified during production at chassis number 0620-0301. Early tailboards had four hinges at the bottom, each one bolted to one of the wooden uprights inside the assembly. These hinges pivoted on blocks welded to the rear cross-member. The inside surface of the tailboard had three rubbing strips that ran from top to bottom, and matching strips running from side to side at the top and bottom, so creating the effect of a raised frame. The later tailboards were mounted quite differently. Instead of hinges, they had a pivot on each side that engaged with the sides of the rear body frame. On the inside surface, they had only the three rubbing strips running from top to bottom and the "frame" effect was absent.

Rover described the upper tailboard, or window section, as the "rear light assembly". It had an aluminium frame and a single-pane glass window that was rubber-glazed to it. (Like the windscreen, it had two panes and a central support on the Tickford prototype.) Three hinges attached it to the upper body cross-member, with woodscrews into the wooden frame there and screws into the window frame. A spring-assisted quadrant was bolted to the body frame on each side, with a knurled nut that tightened a locking screw to hold the window section in the open position. There were some differences between early and late support quadrants, the change being recorded as taking pace at chassis number 0620-0177. There was a nickel-plated lifting handle in the centre of the lower frame rail, with a matching one on the inside to assist in closing the window section.

Roof

The roof panel was made of several sections of BB2 alloy sheet, beaten to shape. The largest was the centre panel. There were then three sections at the front – a canopy panel in the centre, plus right and left corner panels – and three at the rear that were similarly divided. Guttering was fitted all round the roof edges, and concealed many of the nails used to attach the roof sections.

Windscreen and windscreen frame

The wooden frame of the windscreen was attached to the wooden bulkhead side extensions and was raked slightly backwards. The frame was covered in Birmabright sheet that was hand-formed around it, and there were several separate sections – which are not immediately apparent to the eye. There was a single-pane glass windscreen that was unique to the model, and this was rubber-glazed to the frame with a one-piece seal that incorporated a wedge-strip. (Interestingly, the Tickford prototype body on L20 had a divided windscreen.)

Although a ventilator panel below the windscreen was an option for the standard Land Rover, there was no such option for the Station Wagon. The exterior of the bulkhead in the relevant area was neatly panelled, and Rover presumably thought that the opening quarter-lights in the doors would provide sufficient ventilation.

Body floor and wheelboxes

Behind the seats, the back body floor had a support frame of wooden battens. The floor panel itself was a flat sheet of metal, with additional filler panels at the front to meet the base of each door pillar. The overhang at the rear was finished off neatly by a wooden skirt panel that ran right across the back of the vehicle and obscured the top of the rear chassis cross-member.

On either side of this floor was a full-length wheelbox, which not only enclosed the rear wheels but also provided the platform for the rear seats. The section behind each rear wheel was boxed off and there was a hinged flap in the rear face of each wheelbox, with a piano hinge at the top and a spring clip at the bottom to hold it closed. These flaps gave access to the boxed-off areas, which Rover intended as tool boxes. Although they were not lined, each one did have clips to prevent tools sliding about; the left-hand one was furnished with three clips, while the right-hand one had two. These clips were riveted to the inside of each tool box. Both the wheelboxes and the insides of the toolboxes were painted to match the body colour.

Side windows

Each side panel carried a large glass window, divided into two sections. The forward section was fixed in place and was rubber-glazed; the rear was arranged to slide open in an aluminium channel. Each sliding section had a round metal knob bonded to it on the inside at its leading edge, and there was a hinged metal stop on the frame to lock the window closed from the inside.

ELECTRICAL

Trafficators

Semaphore trafficators were fitted as standard to 1950-model Station Wagons for the home market. These were Lucas units, and were let neatly into the trailing edge of each front wing.

Lighting

The first Tickford Station Wagons had five-inch Butler headlamps and a full grille. The seven-inch F700 headlamps and "lights-through" grille were fitted from chassis number 0620-0311 in May 1950. All Station Wagons had the bulkhead-mounted sidelights.

Rear lighting was extremely basic and, in its original form, is now illegal in most countries. The rear number-plate was mounted on a bracket screwed to the centre upright of the

> **PAINT OPTIONS**
>
> The prototype Station Wagon built by Tickford was on pre-production chassis L20, and was later converted to right-hand drive. This vehicle probably had Light Green front panels and a Light Grey body with the swages in Light Green. Some early production models also had this colour scheme.
>
> Other options for the early Station Wagons were Light Green all over, or Light Green lower panels with Light Grey upper panels.
>
> After mid-1949 and the standardisation of Dark Green (Deep Bronze Green) on main-stream Land Rovers, the Station Wagons also became available in all-over Dark Green. Another option was Light Green upper panels and Dark Green below the waist, and some experts claim that a Light Green roof with a Dark Green body was a third option.
>
> When the upper panels were painted in a second colour, the dividing line was above the top swage (just below the side windows), and at the crease below the windscreen. The spare wheel cover was normally painted in the upper colour in these cases. The two-tone paintwork presumably cost extra, although no clear evidence has yet been found.

Minor variations: 1950-season Tickfords for the home market were provided with semaphore trafficators let into the front wings.

FACTORY-ORIGINAL LAND ROVER SERIES I, 80-INCH MODELS

A specially shaped mounting is located centrally for the number-plate, which is illuminated from underneath the D-lamp that provides rear lighting.

tailboard, and this bracket was hinged so that it would hang down below the tailboard when this was open. The idea was that the number-plate would remain visible at all times – an idea that was continued many years later on the first Range Rovers. To this bracket was mounted a Lucas D-lamp, similar to the ones used on standard Land Rovers but in this case with a chromed body rather than a black one.

From the beginning, some export territories required a tail light on each side of the vehicle, and in this case Lucas 488 lamps were fitted to the rear body cross-member below the tailboard. These lamps were in addition to the D-lamp mounted centrally over the number-plate. They carried twin-filament bulbs, one being used for the stop light and the other doubling as the tail light and the direction indicator. Similar bulbs and suitable wiring were fitted to the bulkhead-mounted sidelamps, which then also doubled as flashing indicators.

Control box and fuses

Arrangements for the control box and fuses were the same as on contemporary basic Land Rovers. It nevertheless appears that all the 1951-model Station Wagons had the combined Lucas RF95/2 L2 control and fuse box associated with 1950-season production, and no switch was made to the later RB106/1 type.

Windscreen wipers

Two windscreen wipers were fitted as standard to Station Wagons. They were driven through flexible drive cables by a single wiper motor that was concealed behind the glove boxes at the top of the bulkhead. This motor was a Lucas CR4 G96 type, with Lucas part number 75055. The wiper arms and blades were quite different from those used on standard Land Rovers, the arms having Lucas part number 737573 and the blades part number 727759.

Despite equipment levels that were generally higher than those on the mainstream models, the Tickford Station Wagons were not built with any form of windscreen washer system. Owners have created various systems to meet the legal requirement for one in subsequent years.

INTERIOR

These Station Wagons were configured as seven-seaters, and had a considerably higher level of equipment and finish than the standard Land Rover. The main instrument panel was exactly the same as on the standard Land Rover of the time. The Station Wagons had tool clips low down on the bulkhead to retain the starting-handle. Unlike the mainstream Land Rovers of the time, they also had a conventional rear-view mirror that was screwed to the windscreen header rail. This was in fact the same as the one used on the Rover P3 60 and 75 models of 1948-1949.

Steering wheel, dashboard and controls

The steering wheel on all Station Wagons appears to have been the two-spoke type, even though a four-spoke wheel had become standard on the mainstream Land Rover models in the first half of 1949. There appears to be no rational explanation for this anomaly.

The later handbrake without a Bakelite grip was fitted from R0620-0121 (RHD) and some months later at L0620-0326 (LHD); see the chapter on interior fittings.

The windscreen wiper switch was a push-pull type with a brown Bakelite grip that was mounted on the steering-column shroud, and the direction indicator switch was always a stalk that was mounted on an extension bracket clamped to the steering column. It was the same switch that was used on the 1946-1947 Rover saloons, and it would be logical to conclude that Rover were using up overstocks of the part.

All the 1951-model Station Wagons had the early type of dashboard warning lights with metal bodies (see the chapter on interior fittings), no doubt because their chassis were all early ones. As a result, the later WL3/1 plastic-bodied lights were never fitted. In apparent contradiction of that, however, service literature claims that the longer accelerator pedal cross-shaft was fitted from mid-April 1951 at 1623-0081 and

Tickford created a special upper facia with twin oddments shelves, and trimmed the lower facia in green board. The clips for the starting handle are not fitted on this example.

1626-0021. If that is accurate, it suggests that the chassis were modified before despatch from Solihull.

The later type of bracket for the choke control (see the chapter on interior fittings) was introduced at chassis number 0610-0107 in November 1949, and the modified choke knob and cable assembly that needed no supporting bracket was introduced at 0620-0312 in late April 1950.

On early models, the starting-handle was mounted to the fibreboard lining on the lower bulkhead by two sprung tool clips, but on later ones it was moved to clips on the back of the seat box. It is not clear when this change took place.

Seats (cab)

There were three seats in the cab area of all Station Wagons, and all of them were different from the standard Land Rover seats of the time. Most noticeably, all had curved backrests with two vertical pleats in the covering. This shaped backrest offered a greater degree of comfort than the standard type. All three seats also had the standard wedge-shaped cushions of the period, with a front thigh-roll. Green Vynide upholstery was standard.

The centre and right-hand seats rested on the seatbox, but the left-hand seat (on both left-hand-drive and right-hand-drive models) was quite different and was mounted directly to the floor. It had a tubular frame that ran through pivot brackets attached to the floor at the front, so that the whole seat could be tipped forwards to give access to the rear compartment. The tubular frame was normally painted dark green. The cushion sat in a tray-like structure attached to the tubular frame. On early models, a pocket located on the inboard edge of the tipping front seat was designed to hold the

The passenger's side front seat was mounted on a framework that allowed it to be moved forwards to give access to the rear.

This door trim shows the frame used to hold the main panel in place, the window winder handle, and the door release lever on the window sill. The sticker low down on the door is associated with servicing and is obviously not an original feature. This is the low-mileage original vehicle in Nairobi. (Christopher Race)

The front seats are unique to these models, and have wrap-around backs to provide support.

driver's handbook, but this was deleted from the specification at an unknown point.

Seats (rear)

Four inward-facing seats were fitted above the wheelboxes in the rear of the body. Each pair of seats shared a backrest that was screwed to the wooden side frame just below the window. The four seats were formed by four individual cushions (broadly the same as those for the front seats), which rested in tray-like structures on the wheelbox. Each cushion was restrained by a leather strap that ran from a fastening on the wheelbox to a press-dot fastener on its lower front face. The cushions could also be removed altogether or tilted up and out of the way to give more room for cargo in the rear. In this case, the restraining strap was undone from its dot fastener, the cushion was stood on its back face, and a second leather strap was attached to the dot fastener. This second strap was anchored to the body side behind the backrest.

The Tickford Station Wagons were configured as seven-seaters, and the cushions of the four inward-facing rear seats could be folded up to make more space for cargo. The loose straps seen here hold the cushions in place when lowered.

This photo of a rear seat shows the strap that holds the cushion in place when it is folded up; the same stud on the cushion is used to hold the cushion in place when in the down position, but has not been connected here.

Floor coverings

The Station Wagons came with the luxury of carpet on the gearbox cover. This was shaped to fit and was a mid-green colour with dark green edge binding. Clips held the carpet in place. There was a separate section for the gearbox inspection cover, and this was riveted to the cover itself.

The floor panels in the cab did not have carpet but were covered by rather more practical ribbed black rubber sheeting. There was a single sheet for the right-hand floor, but there were two pieces for the left-hand floor, the second one running under the tipping seat. There was another section of this flooring to cover the floor area between the wheelboxes in the rear. The original rubber sheeting was made by the North British Rubber Company of Fountainbridge, in western Edinburgh. The company no longer exists, having been absorbed into Uniroyal in 1966.

Body trim

Much of the interior of the body was lined with dark green fibreboard, which was mostly screwed to the wooden framework. There were liner panels on the inside behind the doors, and on the rear body sides between these panels and the rear seatbacks. On early models, a dowager strap was attached to the left-hand pillar behind the door, with a woodscrew that passed through it and into the body frame behind. This was intended to make entry to and exit from the rear easier when the left-hand front seat was tipped forwards. It is not clear when the strap was deleted from the specification.

There were also fibreboard liners for each footwell and fibreboard panels on the lower bulkhead below the level of the instrument panel. In this case, the panels were attached to the metal bulkhead by self-tapping screws with cup washers.

Each door had an inner fibreboard liner; on some vehicles these were screwed directly to the door but others appear to have had wood retaining strips that made a neat frame. A chromed window winder handle was mounted high up towards the front of the door, while the door releases had black grips and were mounted through chromed escutcheons on the window ledges towards the rear. Strangely, perhaps, there was neither handle nor strap attached to the door to help pull it closed.

Each door was restrained by a green webbing check strap that was formed in a loop with a flat metal plate over the free ends. This plate was screwed to the dashboard, and the loop was passed over a chromed fitting on the door.

The underside of the roof was also lined, in this case with cream millboard (although there have been reports of green millboard). This was retained by metal strips, one under each roof cross-member, which were screwed through to the wood behind. There was also a large courtesy lamp in the centre of the rear roof, operated by a switch on the body (and not by switches on the doors). This was not listed by Lucas, who made most electrical items for Rover, and it is not clear who manufactured it.

TOOL KIT AND HANDBOOK

Like the mainstream Land Rovers, the Station Wagons were provided with wheel-changing tools, a tyre pump, a starting handle and a set of hand tools in a black hessian roll. The tools were the same as those on the mainstream models, and there were probably similar minor variations from one tool roll to another.

As noted above, the starting handle on early models was mounted to the lower dashboard, but on later models it was relocated on the back of the seat box. The wheelbrace and the jack extension handle were always mounted in tool clips on the back of the seat box, and lay horizontally across the front of the rear passenger compartment.

Further tool clips in the two tool boxes behind the rear wheels provided mountings for the jack handle, the wheelbrace and the tool roll. As explained above, on early Station Wagons the driver's handbook was kept in a pocket beside the left-hand front seat.

THE WELDER

Right from the start of production, Rover could see that their new Land Rover was the ideal basis for a mobile welding plant, and what their own literature initially called the Welding Outfit was displayed on pre-production model number L05 at the Amsterdam Show in April 1948. Production examples did not become available until October 1948, as 1949 models, and by the time of the January 1950 sales brochure, the model was formally known as the Land Rover Mobile Welding Plant.

These were early days, and Rover probably over-estimated the demand for such a vehicle; although it certainly did find customers, it sold only 113 examples in five years (the one on L05 would have made 114 examples), which was an average of just over 22 a year. The Land Rover Welders appear to have been built to order and not for stock.

As with the Tickford Station Wagon, the most important parts of the Welder were actually provided by an outside company (in this case, the Lincoln Electric Company of Welwyn Garden City). So Rover chose to number the Welders in their own chassis sequence. This decision may well have reflected the amount of additional chassis preparation work that was necessary at Solihull, although it is interesting that mobile welders built after the end of 80-inch production were treated as conversions and retained standard chassis numbers. The chassis sequences and detailed production figures are shown in the first chapter of this book, together with those for the mainstream 80-inch models.

Rover sold the Welder fully equipped for arc welding, but oxy-acetylene welding equipment could be added at extra cost, and most known Welders have it. Nevertheless, it was not shown in the "artist's impression" on the cover of the January 1950 sales brochure for the model. The oxy-acetylene equipment included two gas bottles, which were not fitted to the prototype Welder at Amsterdam although the vehicle did have provision for carrying them.

CHASSIS

Early Welders had fishplate brackets welded to the front dumb-irons, exactly like mainstream models. With effect from chassis number 0630-0021, the dumb-irons were simply drilled to receive bolts and the bumper attachment brackets were mounted on the bumper itself.

Up to the end of the 1950 season, all Welders probably 1T8-4 dampers at the front and 1T8-C4 at the rear. Thereafter, they had the 3T8-B1 type at the front and the 4T8-A6 type at the rear. The Welder was fitted with heavy-duty rear springs as standard. The 2½in "wide" front springs with their rear-mounted shackles were not fitted until the start of 1951 Welder production, at chassis numbers 1630-0001 and 1633-0001.

Early Welders had the same freewheel in the driveline as mainstream Land Rovers. The first of the 1951-season Welders still had this, and the change to a selectable four-wheel-drive system was made at chassis numbers 1630-00003, 1633-0002 and 1636-0007.

The earliest welder was pre-production Land Rover L05, which appeared on the Rover stand at Amsterdam in 1948. The large gas bottles, the generator, and the brackets for the welding equipment can be seen here. The welding generator occupied the space that would otherwise have been available for a middle seat.

The gas bottles rested in cradles mounted to a bar that spanned the tailboard opening.

ENGINE

The engine was specially fitted with an eight-blade cooling fan and an oil cooler to prevent overheating when it was driving the arc generator. It also came with an Iso-Speedic engine governor (see the chapter on Optional Equipment) that was supplemented by an additional bellows device manufactured by Lincoln. This was mounted on the engine behind the carburettor and acted as a damper that prevented a sudden rise in engine speed when the load was taken off the welding generator.

The radiator was also fitted with a larger header tank than the standard type, in order to provide additional cooling capacity for when the welding equipment was being used for long periods and the vehicle was, of course, stationary.

TRANSMISSION

The chassis was fitted with a Centre PTO that had the standard triple-pulley arrangement on its output shaft. However, instead of the usual stubby control lever, there was a special cranked lever that gave the necessary clearance from the body of the generator.

BODY

Body specification changes were essentially the same as those for the mainstream Land Rovers, but the Welders had their own changeover points. The "lights-through" grille was introduced after the last of the 1950-season 0630-series Welders had been built, with the result that it first arrived on the 1951 models. Similarly, the wing-mounted sidelamps did not appear on any of the 1951 models but were on the 1952 (and later) models.

All the 0630-series Welders also had windscreen pivots with the castle nut and split pin; none had the unsatisfactory intermediate arrangement, and the 1951 models changed to the type with a locking nut that had by then become standard on mainstream models.

Part of the seatbox centre was cut away on Welders to

make room for the triple vee-belts that took the drive from the PTO pulleys to their counterparts on the arc generator. Lincoln provided a detachable domed housing to protect the area around the belt-drives.

The area above each rear wheelbox was built up to create a stowage box, with a lid hinged from the body capping, and the intention was for these areas to contain items of welding equipment. The prototype and at least one right-hand-drive production Welder also had a step-shaped lidded box over the "nose" of the generator in the centre of the back body, but this seems not to have been made standard.

If the Land Rover was to be used for oxy-acetylene welding as well as arc welding, a special support bar was bolted across the top of the tailboard opening, with a pair of U-shaped brackets on it. Both bar and brackets were probably galvanised. Cradles were then attached to the back of the bar to support the gas cylinders, which were carried at an angle and projected beyond the rear of the vehicle. (The cylinders were not supplied with the Land Rover.) Additional nozzles and gauges for this type of welding were carried in the side lockers.

On the Amsterdam prototype, the supports for the gas cylinders were attached directly to the top of the tailboard and folded down with it. They had adjustable webbing straps to help secure the cylinders. This arrangement was clearly impractical, and was not continued.

ELECTRICAL SYSTEM

On the electrical side, fuse box changes followed those of the mainstream models but all the 0630-series Welders in the 1950 season had the RF95/2 L2 control box with provision for two fuses. In the 1951 season, chassis number 1630-0004 was probably the first one with the new separate fuse-box arrangement, which was of course continued on the 2-litre models for the 1952 and 1953 seasons.

INSTRUMENTS AND CONTROLS

As in other areas of the basic vehicle, the Welders did not deviate from the instrument and control specification used on contemporary mainstream models. However, they had their own changeover points.

The single-piece welded bracket for the choke control was introduced at chassis number 0630-0021, and the smaller third type of bracket was introduced at the start of the 1951 season. The handbrake lever changed from a constant-diameter type to the waisted design at chassis number 0630-0029 on right-hand-drive Welders, but arrived much later on left-hand-drive types, where it did not appear until the start of the 1951 season (at chassis number 1633-0001).

All the 0630-series Welders for 1950 had the earlier type of ribbed speedometer cable, the change to the later type with a smooth casing not being made until the start of 1951-season production. The dashboard warning lights followed the same progression as on mainstream models, but the change to the two-piece plastic type took place at chassis numbers 2630-0007, 2633-0012, and 2636-0001.

SEATS

Early Welders had the same style of seats as their mainstream contemporaries, although of course there was never a centre seat in the cab. All the 0630-series models in the 1950 season had spade-back seats, the change to the shovel-back type taking place at the start of the 1951 season for Welders.

GENERATOR AND WELDING EQUIPMENT

The generator was a self-contained unit that was mounted in the middle of the Land Rover, between and behind the two front seats. It was a Lincoln SA150 type, equipped with three drive pulleys at the rear to suit the Land Rover's PTO arrangements. The generator was also known as a Shield Arc Junior type and was widely available in other configurations. It provided a current of 150 amps and 30 volts.

The Generator was contained within a metal casing that was probably always painted to match the body colour of the Land Rover; examples have been found with both Light Green and Dark Green bodies. The front face of the unit faced the rear of the vehicle and carried a plate on which the two controls were mounted. The control on the left was for the voltage and the one on the right was for the current.

The Lincoln welding unit was available in several different configurations for different vehicles, mostly tractors. For the Land Rover, it was normally painted green.

This 1951 Welder was under restoration when pictured. The Lincoln unit has been trial-fitted but there is still some work to do and the brackets on the right-hand side are missing.

The face-plate was marked with the maker's name and address, the details of the model, and also had an area where the serial number was stamped. Note that similar Lincoln generators were available world-wide and were manufactured in several different countries; the correct Land Rover item was made in Britain and marked appropriately.

There were two threaded studs on the front of the generator casing, and the welding cables would be attached to these when the welder was in use. They appear to have been fitted as standard with wing nuts to secure the cables in place.

The Land Rover Welder was supplied with two 30ft lengths of cable. One was fitted with an attachment lug (for the stud on the casing) and a ground clamp, and the other was a Stable Arc cable with an attachment lug at one end and an electrode holder at the other. When not in use, these two cables could be looped over hooks on the ends of an M-shaped metal support frame that was mounted to the generator casing. A certain amount of arc-welding equipment was supplied with the vehicle, including a face shield, a wire scratch brush, and a chipping hammer.

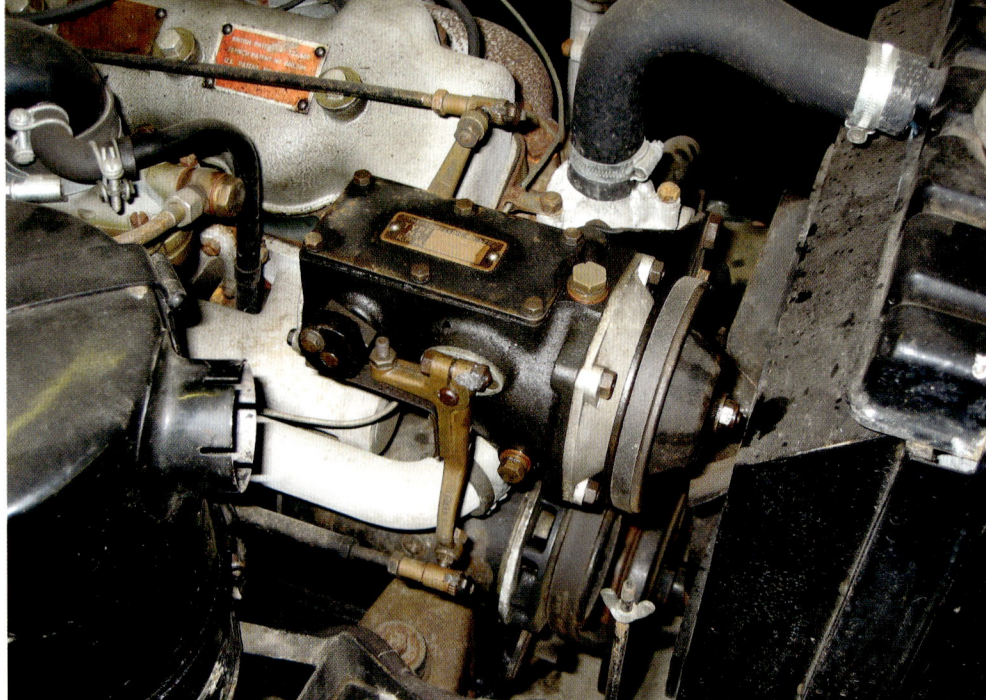

The belt-driven Iso-Speedic engine governor is visible here; the intake for the air cleaner normally obscures it from this angle.

The nose of the welding unit protrudes between the seats. The sliding quadrant below the instrument panel controls the engine speed governor when the welding unit is operating.

The Welder was fitted with an additional bellows control on the governor that prevented a sudden rise in engine speed as the load was taken off the welding generator. It is visible behind the carburettor in this picture.

FIRE ENGINES

The 80-inch fire engine presented a satisfyingly neat profile, especially when fitted with the optional Truck Cab, as on this 1953 model.

Rover recognised the Land Rover's potential as a small fire engine early on. It was small and nimble enough for first-response duties in rural areas and on factory sites, although it was never intended to tackle major fires alone. Pre-production model R06 was built up as a fire engine in 1948, and some brigades, both in Britain and overseas, created their own fire tenders from standard 1.6-litre production Land Rovers. However, the factory-built fire engine did not become available until May 1952, and all those built therefore had the 2-litre engine.

The Land Rover Fire Engine was created as simply as possible, by removing the tailboard, adding a fire pump that occupied the opening for the tailboard and was bolted to the rear of the vehicle, and supplying a number of existing optional extras and a few special parts to complete the installation. Early examples were photographed at the factory with a "three-seater" hood,

but the new Truck Cab option became available from June 1952, and this was commonly but not invariably specified on new Fire Engines. Some fire brigades, especially overseas in places such as New Zealand, added their own modifications to the vehicle as supplied by Rover. Typically, these might include lockers on the rear body sides and a ladder rack.

The Land Rover Fire Engine was considerably more expensive than a basic vehicle, and was priced at £905 in May 1953, with an extra £25 11s 0d for the optional Truck Cab roof. All were painted in Poppy Red, with matching wheels and red upholstery for the seats. Even the backgrounds to the Land Rover alloy badges on the grille and tail panel were sometimes finished in red, although perhaps not by the factory.

Even though Land Rover supplied a standardised product as far as possible, it appears that there may have been minor variations between individual vehicles: different Chief Fire Officers had their own views about what their brigades needed. Where they could not persuade Rover to supply what they wanted, they would often get it manufactured and fitted in their own workshops. The notes in this chapter therefore come with a caution: like those in the chapter on the Tickford Station Wagons, they are generally descriptive rather than prescriptive for a restoration.

CHASSIS

An interesting cosmetic touch was that the chassis frames of all the factory-built Fire Engines were also painted Poppy Red to match the bodywork, although they always had a black fuel tank and tank guard. These "coloured" chassis preceded by more than a year the ones used on the 86-inch Station Wagons from autumn 1953.

The Fire Engine chassis was built with the uprated rear springs as used on Welders and the later Station Wagons, plus 7.00 x 16 tyres. It had a centre power take-off, an oil cooler, a bonnet-mounted spare wheel carrier, an Iso-Speedic engine speed governor, an eight-bladed fan and a 10 psi radiator cap. The oil gauge that always came with the oil cooler was fitted to the pump control panel at the rear rather than to the dashboard, and the engine governor was modified so that it, too, could be operated from the pump control panel.

FIRE PUMP

The fire pump was mounted to the rear chassis cross-member by three long bolts, and to an angled support plate by two more bolts; the support plate was in turn held to the towing plate by four more bolts. The standard pump was made by Pegsons of Coalville in Leicestershire and was their 27H self-priming two-stage impeller type, with an aluminium body and a 200gpm rating. Each pump had a standard 3-inch brass water inlet pipe to British Standard Specification 336, with a screw cap that was attached by a chain. There were two delivery hose outlets on top of the pump, which took a standard British instantaneous coupling and a 2½-inch delivery hose, and a smaller brass pipe leading to the first-aid hose carried on the vehicle. This pipe was routed through the control box for neatness and protection.

The pump was operated from the centre PTO, and the gearbox output flange had an eight-bladed fan bolted to it. There was also a heat shield clamped around the exhaust pipe to keep temperatures down while the vehicle was pumping.

The red finish extended to the inside as well, which was provided from the factory with red seats. Clear here is the hooked slow-running control for use when the vehicle was stationary and the engine was driving the fire pump.

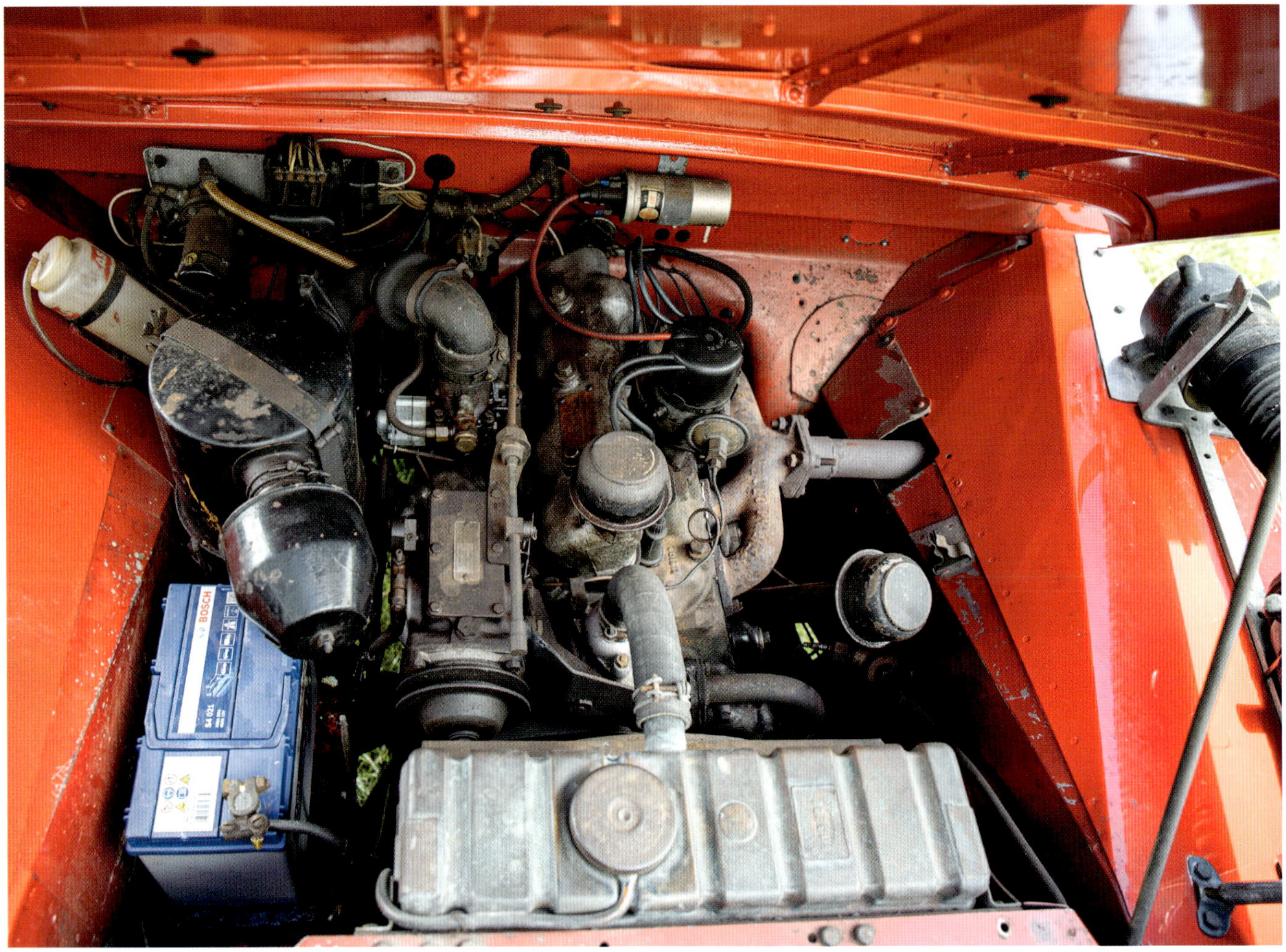

FACTORY-ORIGINAL LAND ROVER SERIES I, 80-INCH MODELS

This is the 2-litre engine in the 1953 fire engine. The engine governor (here missing its drive belt) was standard but did not have the bellows control used on the Welders, which also had a quadrant type governor control inside the cab.

When the metal cab was fitted, the front ladder supports were bolted to it. However, there was no standard design for these supports, and it seems probable that they were fitted by the brigade that owned the vehicle rather than at the factory.

There was considerable variation between one fire engine and the next. This one was built in March 1953 for Windsor Castle, and has a very different type of ladder support as well as a three-stage aluminium ladder instead of a two-stage wooden one. It also has side panniers for firefighting equipment, their canvas covers being rolled back here.

FIRE ENGINES

The standard fire pump was this Pegson 27H type. It was driven from the centre PTO via an overdrive gearbox mounted behind the cross-member.

The control box had three gauges, and turnwheels to control the various functions of the pump.

From the CPTO, a short propshaft with a sliding joint ran to what Rover called an "overdrive gearbox" that was mounted on a carrier bracket attached to the chassis behind the centre cross-member. This reduced the gearbox output speed to suit the operating range of the pump, and a second shaft took the drive from it to the fire pump itself.

CONTROL BOX

A galvanised bracing bar ran across the tailboard aperture between the two rear wheelarches, and was bolted to them immediately below the galvanised cappings on the tail panels. Four bolts held the body of the control box to this bracing bar, to the right of the pump. On the right face of the control box was a second water inlet pipe with protective cover; this would typically be connected to a fire hydrant when the vehicle was pumping water at an incident. The rearward-sloping cover of the control box then contained turnwheel controls for the water valves, plus three gauges.

The water valves often (but not invariably) were identified by red-printed alloy labels riveted to the control box. Typically,

125

above the upper left-hand wheel would be "Pressure pump to first aid hose", below the lower left-hand wheel would be "Suction tank to pump", and above the right-hand wheel "Pressure hydrant to first-aid hose". The three gauges were for engine oil pressure (bottom, black dial), water pressure (white face, reading to 200psi, on the right), and a combined vacuum and pressure gauge (white face, on the left, reading to 30 inches of vacuum and 100psi).

The position of the control box meant that the rear number-plate had to be relocated on right-hand-drive models, and typically it was mounted to the rear-facing edge of the control box itself, with a black Lucas L467 lamp for illumination above it. On left-hand-drive models, the number-plate remained in its usual place on the left tail panel, with the standard arrangements for number-plate illumination.

The engine speed governor control was mounted to the bottom of the control box on a support bracket bolted to the box. This was identical to the dashboard-mounted speed governor control available for other Land Rovers fitted with PTOs, and had a black Bakelite grip. A sheathed control cable ran from the quadrant, along the right-hand chassis side

Different types of label were used over the years. In this case, the turnwheels and the number-plate illumination lamp are missing.

The arrangement of the back body is clear in this picture. The water tank occupies most of the space, making it necessary to mount the fire pump and control panel outboard, while the first-aid hose reel is on a bracket above the tank.

The aluminium hose reel was mounted on a special support bracket that spanned the wheelboxes.

member, and up into the engine compartment, where it was connected in the standard fashion.

LOAD BED

The floor of the load bed was protected by a sheet of marine ply (although in some cases steel plate may have been used). On top of this rested a 40-gallon galvanised steel first-aid water tank, with large filler cap accessible from the rear of the vehicle and its own internal filter. The tank was secured by four transverse metal straps bolted to the wheelarches on each side, and had a rubber mounting pad at each corner to prevented it from chafing against the floor.

Standard equipment included an aluminium hose reel mounted transversely in the load bed above the first-aid tank. This carried a 120-foot length of small-bore red or black rubber hose, with an adjustable brass nozzle. Metal support panels bolted to the wheelarches were braced by a bar running across the top of the first-aid tank, and this bar had a stowage clip for the first-aid hose nozzle. The hose reel was then carried on a pair of triangular legs bolted to the support panel on each side. The side wheels of the original hose reels had the name of Charles Winn & Co Ltd, Birmingham, cast into them.

This picture shows a detail of the hose support bracket, and the oil cooler is visible through the radiator grille. The siren would have been chosen to suit the individual fire brigade; some chose bells.

The hose brackets consisted of a support bolted to the front bumper and braced against the front panel, and a locating bracket on the top of each front wing.

The large-diameter fire hoses were carried on the bonnet in special brackets. Rover provided the brackets but the hoses were chosen by the customer and therefore vary from one fire engine to another.

HOSE SUPPORTS

Rover did not supply suction hoses with the Fire Engine, because their specification varied from one brigade to the next. However, part of the standard equipment was a set of cradles that allowed two interlocking lengths of hose to be carried on the front wings in a U-shape around the bonnet-mounted spare wheel.

Each front wing carried two galvanised hose cradles, bolted through a reinforcing plate that was also pop-rivetted to the top of the wing. There was also a cradle ahead of the bonnet, mounted on a single upright that was bolted to the centre of the front bumper. All the cradles had a strap with a quick-release buckle to hold the hose in place.

Delivery hoses were normally carried in the back body, either on the wheelboxes or between the fire pump and the hose reel. Again, individual fire brigades specified their own types, and so Rover did not supply these hoses with the vehicle. Nevertheless, the company did supply Pyrene type MFG5 mechanical foam generators as an extra-cost option, for fitting to either or both of the main delivery hoses.

OPTIONAL EQUIPMENT

Rover always envisaged the Land Rover as a basic platform to which customers could fit whatever extras they chose. When the vehicle was launched in 1948, doors, a passenger seat, a spare wheel, sidescreens, and the three-seater tilt were all extra-cost options.

By October 1948, these items were incorporated in the basic price of the Land Rover, but there were more new options. The handbook lists trafficators (semaphore turn signals), a bonnet-mounted spare wheel carrier, a chaff guard, a towing plate and towing jaw with extension, and a special towing plate suitable for use with a combine harvester. In addition, there were power take-offs (PTOs) for the rear and for the centre of the vehicle.

Over the years, Rover built on this basic concept, and there was a very large selection of optional equipment available by the time the 80-inch models gave way to 86-inch types in 1953. Some of this could be fitted on the assembly lines, but other items were for the dealer or the customer to fit as appropriate.

Bonnet mount for spare wheel

To make more room in the back body, the spare wheel could be mounted on the bonnet. This option was available from very early on, and was in fact displayed on the Amsterdam show stand vehicle in April 1948. However, customer availability may not have been before October 1948. There

The Brockhouse trailer was supplied in a colour to match the Land Rover that was to tow it. This is an early Light Green example.

OPTIONAL EQUIPMENT

were two types available, one to suit the standard 6.00x16 tyre size and the other to suit the wider 7.00x16 option.

The bonnet mount consisted of a galvanised dome attached to the bonnet by means of rivets; this both supported the wheel and strengthened the bonnet panel. There were four rubber support blocks, mounted at 3 o'clock, 6 o'clock, 9 o'clock and 12 o'clock, and there was a securing rod that fitted into a slot in the mounting dome and held the wheel in place by means of a clamp. The only difference between the two sizes of bonnet mount was that the one for the 7.00 tyres incorporated an additional support block for the wheel clamp.

Brockhouse trailer

Rover recognised early on that the Land Rover had limited carrying capacity in the body but could transport considerably more if towing a trailer. Trailers were not in the Rover Company's repertoire, but J Brockhouse & Co Ltd of nearby West Bromwich specialised in their manufacture. By late November 1948 a prototype trailer was ready and was pictured at Solihull.

The agreement with Brockhouse was that Rover would supply these trailers as an item of extra equipment (with Rover option number E27), and the first production example reached Solihull in April 1949. On its introduction, the trailer was priced at £75. There is a suggestion that the later trailers were not actually built by Brockhouse but that their construction was sub-contracted to another company in the Midlands.

Mounted on the drawbar were a handbrake, a support leg, and a damped trailer hitch. Parts of the handbrake mechanism can also be seen here.

BROCKHOUSE TRAILER IDENTIFICATION

Every Brockhouse trailer has a black printed brass or aluminium maker's plate attached to the draw bar, and into this is stamped the trailer's identification number. The Brockhouse system was to use a single numbering sequence for all types of trailer, and to add a prefix identifying the type. Brockhouse knew the Land Rover trailer as their BT8 type.

The earliest known Land Rover trailer has serial number BT8/4260, and could perhaps be the prototype. The last example was built in 1965 with number BT8/16666, and research suggests that 977 of these trailers were built in just over 25 years.

The Rover despatch records for the trailers include one final entry, which is for a LoLode trailer numbered CA 11655578. This trailer was a special order for SB Wilks that was delivered to him at the Lode Lane factory in 1965. It was not a final Brockhouse delivery, but the clerk responsible entered it in the Brockhouse trailers book as there was no other obvious place to do so!

Identification plates were mounted on the trailer draw bar.

When cleaned up, the main identification plate looked like this. (Jim Macri)

A typical early arrangement is seen here, with a large T plate and a single rear D-lamp to illuminate the offset number-plate.

In this case, the trailer was supplied in Bronze Green.

The Brockhouse trailer was rated to carry 15cwt (3180 lb, 1442kg) and had been designed specifically for use with the Land Rover. It therefore ran on Land Rover wheels and tyres, and its wheel track was identical to the Land Rover's, so that the trailer could more easily follow the towing vehicle over rough terrain. There were some major changes in the design of the trailer in July 1955, during the currency of the 86-inch Land Rovers.

The basis of the Brockhouse trailer was a simple chassis made from welded steel bars. Below this were mounted semi-elliptic springs, each two inches wide and with seven leaves. The springs were anchored at the front end and shackled at the rear. The axle was a simple 1.5-inch square steel bar, and on each end was a drop-forged steel hub with roller bearings. Rods linked to an over-run mechanism on the draw bar operated eight-inch twin-shoe drum brakes. The brakes could also be applied by a handbrake on the draw bar that acted on the same rods. Minor changes were made to the brake shoes and backplates after trailer number BT8/9301.

On the early (pre-July 1955) trailers, the spring shackle plates were shaped cast items, there were grease nipples in the ends of the spring eye pins, and each hub grease cap had a hexagon-head screw. Later trailers had plain spring shackle plates, no nipples in the spring pins (although some had grease nipples in the spring eye itself) and simple push-fit hub grease caps, without a screw fixing.

The draw bar extended forwards from the chassis and carried an adjustable support leg. The coupling at its front end was either an eye-type or a ball-type, and would slide in its housing to operate the trailer brakes. On the early (pre-July 1955) trailers, the coupling had an oval release handle and its mounting was held to the draw bar by four bolts that passed through separate cylinders cast into the edge of the ring. From BT8/12325 in July 1955, there was a simple bar-type handle with a serrated lower edge, and the bolts securing the coupling housing to the drawbar were no longer in separate housings.

The handbrake on the drawbar also differed between early and late trailers. Early ones had a narrow grip, but later grips had a serrated lower edge and a securing loop. When a ball-type coupling was fitted, the trailer came with a tow ball of the appropriate 2-inch diameter for bolting to the rear cross-member of the towing vehicle. (Note that these towing balls are larger than the modern standard 50mm size and are perfectly spherical; the modern 50mm ball has a flattened top surface.)

The body was an all-steel open box type, with a 16swg floor panel and 18swg sides and ends with pressed swages for strength. These swages were distinctive, with a diagonal pressing behind and in front of each wheel, and a cross-shaped pressing on the front panel and tailgate, in each case with a circular centre pressing as well. The top of each body panel was rolled over a reinforcing steel rod, and cut-outs in the sides allowed a canvas cover to be tied in place over the rod. The tailboard pivoted at the top so that the trailer could be used for tipping, and at the bottom it was held shut by retaining pins on chains. There was no provision for drainage, and as a result the Brockhouse trailer has always been very vulnerable to rust.

A simple domed steel mudguard was bolted to each side panel, and on trailers built before 1954 the single tail light was carried on an angled bracket attached to the rear. This light was the same as those on the Land Rover of the time: early trailers had Lucas D-lights, turned through 90 degrees so that the curved top faced away from the trailer. (New regulations in 1954 in Britain required two tail lights to be fitted to the trailer.) The whole of each trailer (unless to special order) was painted to match the towing Land Rover. The very first examples therefore had Light Green body and chassis, and these remained available into 1950 even though the Land Rover switched to Deep Bronze Green in summer 1949. This was presumably because a stock of trailers had been built up with the early colour finish. Later ones did change to Deep Bronze Green.

In Britain, trailers built up to 1954 would have had a rectangular number-plate on the tailboard along with a square plate bearing the letter T in white with reflective red studs; some had T-shaped plates. Later ones would have had a triangular trailer plate on the tailboard, again with reflective red studs on a white background.

In Britain, some examples with special bodywork were supplied to the Ministry of Supply (probably for Army use), to the Civil Defence organisation, to the Auxiliary Fire Service and to other fire brigades. The special features available included a canvas tilt supported by a special tilt frame that slotted into uprights bolted on the inner surfaces of the body sides. Some of the Civil Defence trailers were for Field Cable Party units whose task was to lay emergency telephone lines, and these were fitted with a cable reel on a support frame bolted through the floor to a threaded plate on an additional cross-member. Those ordered by fire brigades had a variety of additional fixings and stowage lockers for hoses and firefighting equipment.

Capstan (front) winch

A capstan-type front winch became available in late summer or autumn 1950 (some sources say August, others claim October). This was made for Rover by Aeroparts of Hereford, and was introduced to replace the earlier rear-mounted capstan winch that had proved troublesome in service. Both types of winch could be supplied with a special wrench that fitted the bollard screw. These winches had serial numbers that reflected their association with the Land Rover, and were numbered from 86-0001 onwards.

The front winch was mounted on a thick steel plate bolted between the bumper and the no 2 chassis cross-member and was driven by a shaft from the front PTO; a dog clutch on the crankshaft vibration damper was engaged by a lever next to the bollard. The mounting plate and the capstan itself were normally painted black but the centre plate around the capstan was left unpainted. A control rod with a black grip protruded through the support pate and a sturdy fairlead (rope guide) was bolted to the bumper.

This winch shared many parts with the earlier rear-mounted capstan winch and had the same 2500 lb line-pull rating. It could be ordered as a factory-fitted option or as a kit to be fitted at a later stage. Whether fitted at the factory or at a later date, the installation required five distance tubes to be inserted into the no 2 cross-member so that this was not distorted when the winch fixing bolts were tightened. However, these bolts were later replaced in the kits by riv-nuts.

Aeroparts made three versions of this winch over the ten years they built it. The earliest version, which is appropriate to the 80-inch (and 86-inch) models, has four drain grooves in the lip surrounding the bollard; the aluminium gear casing has rounded front and rear edges and is stamped with a four-digit serial number prefixed by AEH.V. The first 200 of these winches had a slightly different size of needle roller bearing supporting the rear of the worm gear; on later ones, the gear casing was modified to suit the new size of bearing.

The Land-Rover Centre Power Take-Off

THE Centre Power Take-off of the Land-Rover is designed for driving special mobile portable plant carried in the body of the vehicle such as milking appliances, air compressors, spraying machines, electric generators, etc. The driving pulley has three grooves for Vee belts and is located at the forward end of the rear power take-off driving shaft. It is controlled by a lever and knob mounted on top of the main gear box.

For price see overleaf

This 1949 sales leaflet for the Centre PTO illustrates the layout of components very well. The short control lever emerged between the seats; a special cranked handle was used on Welders to give clearance in front of the welding generator unit.

The combined water temperature and oil pressure gauge could be fitted neatly into the blanking plate for the unused steering column position.

Neat tubing – with plenty of coils to absorb vibrations – runs to the back of the combined gauge.

Centre PTO

A centre PTO could be fitted to power equipment mounted on the Land Rover, and would typically be fitted with a multi-belt pulley or with a shaft to drive machinery mounted on the vehicle. Its drive came through a dog clutch on the rear of the gearbox mainshaft, and was engaged by a lever that emerged through the centre of the seatbox between the seats. Inevitably, the centre seat had to be removed to permit this.

Chaff guard

The chaff guard was probably introduced around summer 1949, and the earliest known photograph dates from June that year. It was a fine mesh screen that was fitted between the radiator grille and the grille panel, and was held in place by the grille securing bolts. Its purpose was to prevent the radiator becoming clogged when the vehicle was used for farm work such as reaping.

There were three different types, to suit the full grille, the lights-through grille, and the inverted T grille. All of them seem to have remained rare.

Combined water and oil gauge

A combined water temperature and oil pressure gauge was available and was typically used on vehicles used for prolonged periods of stationary running, as often occurred when the PTOs were in use. This instrument was made by Jaeger and had the usual white markings on a black face, with white needles. The top half of the gauge showed water temperature and the lower half showed the oil pressure.

The gauge was typically fitted to the bulkhead on the left-hand side of the main instrument panel on both right-hand-drive and left-hand-drive models, because this position provided the simplest runs for the associated cabling and tubing. Dealers and owners found a variety of ways of securing it to the bulkhead, but one neat option on right-hand-drive models was to make use of the blanking plate that covered the redundant opening in the bulkhead for the left-hand drive steering column.

Compressor

The Land Rover could be adapted as a mobile compressor, and the appropriate conversion was available by December 1949. The air compressor itself was mounted in the back body on a steel bedplate that was bolted to the chassis frame through anti-vibration mounts. It was a two-stage three-cylinder type, manufactured by Alfred Bullows & Son Ltd of Walsall as their 2A 500 model.

The compressor was driven by triple vee-belts from the centre PTO. An oil cooler was a recommended fitment if the Land Rover was to be used in hot climates, and became standard with the compressor later on.

Cool-ride seat pad

This presumably was a pad that allowed air to circulate through the cushion section of the seat, but there is very little information available about it.

Crop Sprayers

Two specialist companies developed crop-spraying attachments in the early days of the Land Rover. These were the Dorman Sprayer Company of Cambridge and E Allman & Co Ltd of Chichester.

Dorman had a crop sprayer attachment ready for the Land Rover from early on, and developed the prototype on pre-production Land Rover number L17. This attachment was known as the Dorman-Simplex Crop Sprayer and initially cost £107 10s 0d.

A tank was mounted in the body of the Land Rover to carry the liquid for spraying, and a pump driven from the centre PTO delivered the liquid under pressure to the spray booms. The booms were mounted on an angle-iron framework and were designed to fold upwards for transport. When in use, the booms

The Alfred Bullows Compressor was a very rare option that was driven from the Centre PTO.

An eight-bladed fan and special cowl were introduced on later models to keep temperatures under control in stationary running. This one is on a 1953 fire engine.

were lowered and projected from the side of the vehicle; they were spring-loaded to prevent damage if they hit an obstruction.

The Allman sprayer was known as the Plantector, and in this case the tank was mounted at the back of the vehicle in the tailboard opening, and was supported on two angled arms that were bolted to the drawbar. The pump was driven from the centre PTO, and there were twin spray booms. These could be raised for transport.

Cutter bar

Whatley Brothers took over a long-established small iron foundry in Bucklebury, Berkshire in 1947 and among their early products was a cutter bar for mowing that could be attached to the driver's side of the Land Rover. The bar had a length of 5ft and was made to be easily detachable. It was probably belt-driven from the centre PTO.

Engine governor

Some uses of the Land Rover as a stationary power source required a greater degree of engine speed control than could be achieved with the standard adjustment lever on the dash, and from April 1949 an auxiliary engine governor was made available. This was manufactured by the Iso-Speedic Company of Warwick and the Land Rover version had their model number 545/4.

The governor itself was contained in a steel box with a black chemical finish and a drive pulley at the front. All examples had an identification plate on the top face, initially made of brass but later made of alloy. The assembly was mounted on a bracket attached to the engine thermostat housing, and the governor was driven by a belt from the water pump pulley. The two lower fixing holes in the mounting bracket were slotted to give a limited amount of adjustment and achieve the correct belt tension. There was a rod connection to the throttle linkage.

A second rod connected the governor to the operating lever, which was on a quadrant mounted to the bulkhead below the instrument panel. This quadrant had 12 notches, each one representing about 150rpm of engine speed. With the control lever fully over to the left, the governor was off, and when fully over to the right it would hold the engine speed at about 3000rpm.

There were two types of governor for the 80-inch models. On engines up to and including 86-1871, there was a straight accelerator pump rod, and on these engines it was necessary to change the carburettor and modify the fan cowl when fitting the governor. On later engines, the governor had a cranked rod, there was a cam and spring, and the fitting was more straightforward.

The thermostat housing on early engines had a pair of bolts onto which the support bracket for the governor was mounted, and early engines also had a double fan pulley to take the drive belt for the governor. However, during the 1950 season a different thermostat housing was fitted and a single fan pulley was fitted. So if a governor was fitted to engines subsequent to number 061-12001, the early type of thermostat housing had to be fitted, along with a double fan pulley. Later engines had stud fixings on the mounting bracket for the governor, and the second pulley that was added to them differed from the early type and was accompanied by a distance washer.

Note that the Iso-Speedic engine governor was not the same thing as the Iso-Speedic road speed governor, which was designed in conjunction with the Rover Company to suit the later OHV engines and did not become available until 1961.

Flag staff

It was presumably military demand that led to Rover supplying a flag staff for the 80-inch Land Rover. The staff was a short chromed pole that could be bolted to the front of the bonnet.

Floor mats

Rover made floor mats available for the 80-inch models, and these were always of the rubber link type. There were driver's and passenger's side mats to suit both right-hand-drive and left-hand drive vehicles. In addition, there were floor mats for the back body, one covering the full length of the floor (for when the spare wheel was carried on the bonnet) and another with a cutout to fit around the spare wheel when it was carried in the back.

Foot support for accelerator

A foot support for the accelerator pedal was available, which was essentially a rubber pad secured to the bulkhead by four drive screws. It was only made available for right-hand drive models.

Front PTO

A third power take-off option became available in October 1950, which allowed power to be taken from the nose of the crankshaft. This was typically used to power a front-mounted winch, which at the time would almost invariably have been a capstan type.

This system depended on a modified vibration damper fitted to the nose of the crankshaft. The modification was essentially a dog clutch, and power was transmitted through a short propshaft to the driven accessory. There was a hand control for engaging and disengaging the dog clutch.

Fume curtain

The third type of hood, introduced in January 1950, could be accompanied by a partition or fume curtain behind driver. This was a separate canvas panel that contained two rectangular windows; these were probably made of gauze on the first examples but later changed to celluloid. The fume curtain was attached to the front hoodstick by webbing straps and buckles, three at the top and two on each side, with two more at the bottom that attached the curtain to the body.

The fume curtain was only suitable for use with these later hoods, and it was probably for that reason that what would now be called an aftermarket conversion was brought to market in early 1951. Spiller & Wilkins, a large agricultural haulage company based at Chilmark near Salisbury, introduced a wooden partition incorporating a rear window that fitted between the seats and the back body. The panel was made of plywood with a polished mahogany finish and cost £6 6s 0d. It probably only ever attracted buyers in the area around Salisbury itself.

Guard rails

A hooped guard rail could be bolted through the body capping on either side of the tailboard opening. This was designed to prevent passengers sitting in the rear (whether on the wheelboxes or on the proper rear seats) from falling out of the vehicle. These guard rails had become available by October 1948, and would therefore have been fitted to several vehicles before the proper rear seats became available in late summer 1949.

Heater and heater-demister

No heater or demister was provided as standard for the 80-inch Land Rover, but during 1949 it became possible to buy a heater as an optional extra. This first type of heater had no provision for windscreen demisting and was manufactured by the Clayton Dewandre Company of Lincoln, who also made similar heaters for a variety of commercial vehicles, together with vacuum braking equipment.

Like many other Clayton heaters of the time, the one for the Land Rover was essentially a round box with vanes and flaps to give some directional distribution for its heat. Original heaters had a grey-green metallic stove-enamelled finish; the Clayton Classics division still makes and repairs these heaters today, although they are normally prepared with a silver gunmetal finish. There was a triangular maker's badge attached to the front of the heater box, reading "Clayton Type CB".

The heater itself was normally mounted on the cab side of the bulkhead, just above the bellhousing cover and offset towards the left-hand side. Two metal pipes ran from the back of the unit and passed through the bulkhead, with appropriate grommets to prevent fretting. They were connected by rubber hoses to metal inlet and outlet pipes that ran to the thermostat housing, which on early engines was tapped for the purpose. Coolant from the engine circulated through the heater to provide heat. There was also a stopcock (usually painted red) on the outlet pipe from the thermostat so that the heater could be cut out of the coolant circuit in hot weather.

The Clayton heater normally has a very long service life, and the all-copper wire-wound tubes of its heat-exchanger core resist blockages and leaks. Some Clayton heaters were fitted with bleed screws, but the majority were not, and bleeding was achieved as part of the normal process of purging the cooling system of air.

Early in the 1953 season, Rover began to supply a Smith's heater unit in place of the Clayton type. This had a generally similar appearance but its body was finished in black. It also had fittings for demister outlets, which were introduced as a kit of parts slightly later. The demister assembly simply had black bellows-type hoses that ended in fishtail outlets that could be bolted to the windscreen frame. Rover Service literature claimed that the Smith's heater was introduced at chassis numbers 3610-0134, 3613-0225, and 3616-0090, although it was obviously possible to fit the new heater and its demister assembly retrospectively to an older vehicle as well.

Heavy-duty springs

Heavy-duty rear springs were an option that was required when the rear of the Land Rover was permanently loaded, as in the case of the Compressor. They had a 300 lb rating and were fitted as standard to the Welder from the beginning and to the Station Wagon from the start of the 1950 season.

Hesford winch

CM Hesford & Co Ltd, of Ormskirk in Lancashire, offered a heavy-duty winch for the Land Rover, designed for tree pulling and other jobs that required a particularly powerful pull. Very little information is available about this winch, which was mounted to the rear of the Land Rover, bolted to the drawbar and probably to the rear cross-member as well. It appears to have been driven from the rear PTO. A ground anchor or trail was lowered to maintain stability, and the winch cable was paid out through a fairlead mounted above this.

Hesford went on to supply heavy-duty trailer-mounted winches for similar purposes, which were designed to be towed behind the Land Rover.

Oil cooler and temperature gauge

From late in 1950, an oil cooler was made available to keep the engine temperature under control during prolonged stationary work. It was possible to fit this to existing models as well.

The cooler itself consisted of seven wound coils in a simple metal frame that was bolted to the cross-member in front of the radiator at the bottom and to the radiator itself at the top. Its inlet pipe ran back to the oil pump, and its outlet pipe ran to a banjo bolt on the side of the sump.

The oil cooler always came with a higher-capacity oil pump, which in practice was the type that had been fitted to the six-cylinder engine in the Rover P3 75 saloon. The kit came with an eight-blade fan that was accompanied by an appropriate cowl, a 15psi radiator cap (instead of the standard 4psi type), and an oil temperature gauge. This gauge was tapped into a sender unit bolted to the left-hand inner wing and was usually let into the bulkhead to the left of the instrument panel, although there appears to have been some inconsistency about this. This position gave the simplest run for the wiring running from the sender unit to the gauge, and was normally used on left-hand-drive vehicles as well as on right-hand-drive types.

Two types of oil cooler assembly were made available, with minor differences between them. The later type was introduced during the 1951 season to suit engines numbered from 1610-2272 and 1613-1649.

The oil cooler was accompanied by an oil temperature gauge that was usually fitted to the bulkhead alongside the main instrument panel.

Pedal pads

The brake and clutch pedals came as standard with a series of pips on their faces to give additional grip for a boot or shoe, but in some cases this proved inadequate. So by 1949 Rover had introduced the option of rubber pedal pads for these two pedals (there was never one for the accelerator pedal). The ribbed pads were bonded to a steel backing pad and lugs on this pad had to be bent over and around the pedals to secure the rubber in place.

Radiator muff

Oyler was a London company that specialised in making radiator muffs for a variety of vehicles. These were lightly padded and normally had a black leather outer covering. The one for the Land Rover stretched across the full width and depth of the radiator grille, and was held to the grille itself by 10 metal clips. It was made with openings for the headlights. The centre panel could be rolled up to give maximum airflow, and when rolled down could be secured by press studs on either side. It seems to have remained very rare.

Radio

Radios were uncommon even in saloon cars when the first 80-inch models left the factory in 1948, but by mid-1951 customer expectations were changing and a radio was offered as an optional extra for the 1952 models. It could obviously be fitted retrospectively to earlier Land Rovers as well.

Two types of valve radio were made available, one with Medium Wave and Long Wave reception, and the other with Short Wave and Medium Wave reception. Both were probably manufactured by HMV. Radios were mounted to the bulkhead on a simple bracket, typically outboard of the driver with the control panel angled upwards for easy visibility. A radio speaker would be mounted to the bulkhead on the inboard side of the steering wheel, and the aerial was mounted to the front wing (on the driver's side to reduce the length of cabling needed) with the aid of a bracket, which differed between right-had-drive and left-hand-drive applications.

Suppressor units were available for the spark plugs (see below), the distributor king lead, and the condenser, coil, dynamo, pump and wiper motor A suppressed voltage control box was also listed for cases of need.

Rear bench seats

Inward-facing rear bench seats that were mounted on top of the wheelboxes became available over the summer of 1949, and were probably designed initially to meet the requirements of the large order for the British armed forces that had been placed. However, it appears that these seats were not available on civilian models before March 1951, and they were always for export only, because Rover feared the loss of the Land Rover's exemption from Purchase Tax in Britain if it was re-classified as a passenger-carrying vehicle.

Each seat consisted of a galvanised steel backrest frame that was bolted to the wheelbox, with an outward-facing backrest panel that was painted to match the bodywork. A galvanised steel lower frame pivoted from this and retained the cushion. Each seat could therefore be folded up to leave extra space for cargo in the back body, and each cushion section could be retained in the upright position by a webbing strap that was pop-riveted to the front of the seat base and had a hook that

Pictured here on a 1950-model 80 that was new to the British Army are the inward-facing rear seats and the hooped handrails that went with them. It is clear here why the spare wheel was better carried on the bonnet when these seats were in use!

engaged with the body side capping. Both parts of each seat had a one-piece cushion that was upholstered in green Vynide to match the seats in the cab.

When these seats were in use, the spare wheel had to be removed from the back body and mounted on the optional bonnet carrier. Rover recommended fitting the guard rails with them, for the safety of the rear passengers. As the March 1951 sales leaflet explained, "these removable seats will be found particularly useful when fitted to a Land-Rover having a metal detachable top, for converting it into an all enclosed weatherproof passenger carrying vehicle."

Thicker cushions were fitted to these seats from mid-May 1952, and the strap that holds the seat upright was lengthened by an inch to suit. This change took place with effect from chassis numbers 2610-5266, 2613-4674, 2616-3184, 2663-1180 and 2666-1009 (a Home market number is included because the seats were fitted to British military Land Rovers numbered in the 2610-series).

The non-availability of these seats in Britain prompted J&L White, a coach trimming company in Leeds, to introduce their own rear seats for the Land Rover. In this case, the backrest panel was clamped to the hoodsticks, which had to be erected. The cushions and backrests of these seats were manufactured from latex foam over a plywood base, and were upholstered in green.

Rear winch

The first winch introduced as a Land Rover extra was a capstan type that was driven from the rear PTO. Numbered as optional extra E11, it was manufactured by Aeroparts of Hereford. The winch mounted directly to the PTO casing by means of lugs and four studs, and was designed to suit the later six-spline output shaft. Rope speed was dependent on the gear selected and the winch could be controlled by using the Land Rover's clutch. Rover Service Bulletins note that by transposing the PTO gears, a different range of rope speeds could be achieved.

The earliest sales leaflet for this winch is dated January 1950, and shows a cost of £20 in addition to the £26 for the PTO itself. However, the winch proved unsatisfactory in service. The attachment lugs on the alloy winch casing were not strong enough to take the strain, especially if the winch was overloaded, and it was impossible to tell when the mechanism had reached its tolerance limit. The shear pin was designed to protect against overload, but in practice the mounting lugs often fractured as well.

It looks as if Rover had given up on this winch by October 1950, when they began to offer instead a front-mounted capstan type that was also made by Aeroparts and shared several components with the original rear-mounted winch. Nevertheless, the rear-mounted winch seems to have remained available until May 1955, when the stocks held by Rover ran out. Low demand was clearly a barrier to further production, but theoretically, at least, spare parts remained available for some time afterwards.

These winches had an identification number stamped into their casings. The first ones had a three-digit serial number with an AEH prefix, and later ones had an AEH.A prefix with a three-digit serial number followed by A.

Rear PTO

Maurice Wilks' original vision of the Land Rover was as a vehicle that could duplicate many of the roles of a farm tractor, and among those roles was that of stationary power source. To transfer power from the vehicle to whatever piece of farm machinery it had to drive, there had to be a readily-accessible power take-off.

The rear power take-off (RPTO) was manufactured for the Rover Company by Aeroparts of Hereford, who also made capstan winches for the Land Rover. Unlike the winches, these did not carry Aeroparts serial numbers but had Rover ones, which began at 86-0001. Each PTO consisted of a simple gearbox that was bolted to the rear cross-member. Its input side was connected to the centre power take-off (CPTO) by a propshaft that ran above the axle and passed through the large circular aperture in the cross-member and into the back of the PTO unit. Drive was then transferred from a gear on the input side to a second gear that provided the output. The output was through a short shaft.

The first 400 RPTO units had a 10-spline output shaft, but this restricted the Land Rover's use because most farm machinery of the time was made to suit the six-spline output

The rare capstan winch for the rear PTO.

The rear PTO is installed here with the belt pulley that enabled it to drive certain types of farm machinery. An extended towing plate is bolted to the drawbar, and a pintle jaw is in turn bolted to the towing plate.

The serial number of each rear PTO unit was stamped into the top of the main casing.

shaft that had been adopted as standard during the 1930s. So from number 86-0401 all RPTO units had a six-spline output shaft. Soon after the six-spline type entered production, which was probably around autumn 1949, the gearbox casting was changed. The breather was moved from its original position directly above the input gear to an extension casting on its left, an oil drain plug was added, and the original strengthening webs were removed.

The RPTO could be supplied with just an output shaft (when a protective cowl was also supplied), or with a belt pulley or drive flange that mounted over the shaft. The belt pulley was designed for use with the flat 8-inch wide belts that were commonly used to drive agricultural machinery, and the first 400 examples were made to suit the original ten-spline output shaft; later ones were obviously made to suit the six-spline type. The protective cowl was made of galvanised steel and had an inspection hole in its top surface, and later ones had a slot to take a removable rear cover plate. (There was also an early type, associated with the pre-production models, that was smaller and more box-like.)

In November 1949, the RPTO drive unit was priced at £20 and the pulley added a further £15. Rover insisted that an engine speed governor was essential as well, and that added a further £15 to the cost. Later, an oil cooler was also recommended as a desirable extra with the RPTO.

Rover Service Bulletins pointed out that a different set of

OPTIONAL EQUIPMENT

The early type of PTO guard looked like this one, seen on a pre-production model.

The split-rim wheels were normally painted in exactly the same way as the standard types.

output speeds could be obtained from the RPTO by swapping the gears: instead of the standard 5:6 ratio, a ratio of 6:5 could then be achieved, although inevitably with a proportionate loss of torque at the output shaft. The RPTO remained available for many years after the end of 80-inch Land Rover production, and its design remained unchanged until 1968.

Spark plug suppressors

Suppressors were an option that was mostly found on vehicles fitted with a radio. The suppressors were black plastic units that screwed in between the plug lead nuts and the shrouds.

Speedometer with tenths of a mile

A speedometer with a tenths of a mile readout on the elapsed mileage counter was a very uncommon optional extra.

Split-rim wheels

Military-pattern split-rim wheels were made available by November 1948, if not earlier. They always had a 16-inch diameter and a 5-inch rim, to suit the wider tyres often required on military vehicles. The two halves of each wheel were held together by eight bolts, and there was a rubber gaiter running around the rim inside the tyre to prevent the inner tube chafing on the join in the rim. These rims were never very common, were not confined exclusively to military vehicles, and were

FACTORY-ORIGINAL LAND ROVER SERIES I, 80-INCH MODELS

The split-rim wheel's two halves were clamped together by the eight bolts.

kit was announced in the June 1957 Service Bulletin. This was designed to suit all models and could be retro-fitted to the 80-inch Land Rover.

Towing attachments

Several different towing attachments were available to suit the variety of arrangements on the agricultural equipment of the time.

The basic Towing Plate was a stepped steel plate that was held to the drawbar by two bolts. It was supplied with 1in distance pieces so that the towing height could be varied. At the opposite end, the tow ball could be mounted through a single hole in the horizontal surface; this hole had a diameter of 7/8in (22.2mm). For Land Rovers fitted with a six-spline adapter for the rear PTO, Rover supplied a longer towing plate to give the necessary clearance.

An alternative was a Pintle Pin and Bracket. This consisted of a jaw-type bracket that was bolted to the centre of the rear cross-member, with a standard pintle pin passing through it; the pin was retained by a chain. In cases where the presence of a rear PTO made this mounting impossible, Rover supplied an L-shaped plate that bolted to the cross-member, and the pintle jaw could be bolted to this.

The special Combine Harvester Towing Plate was available only to order. It was a cranked triangular plate with two holes in its face rather than just one, and bolted to the drawbar.

A Towing Jaw could be ordered, with angled jaws that held a pintle pin and securing chain, and a version of this with straight jaws could also be had. A third version had a curved face at the back of the jaws and a pintle pin that had a handle on top and the usual securing chain.

certainly not fitted to all the 80-inch models delivered to the British Army – although some did have them.

Swivel pin gaiter kit

Gaiters for the front swivels were not available as a factory option during the production life of the 80-inch models, but a

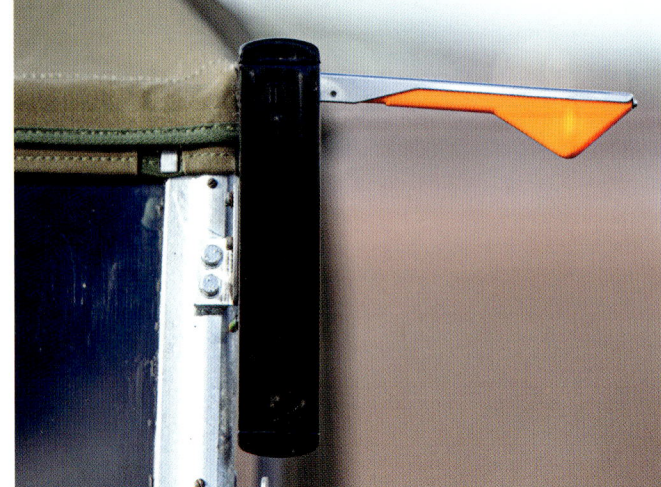

The Lucas trafficators were mounted at the top of each windscreen pillar.

This is the mounting on a 1950 model, showing the bracket bolted to the windscreen pillar.

OPTIONAL EQUIPMENT

Trailer electrical connections
To suit the standard three-pin trailer plug mounted on the rear cross-member, Rover supplied a matching three-pin electrical socket to be mounted on the trailer, and this came from the factory with 12ft of cable. This cost extra on the first Land Rovers, but after October 1948 was supplied as standard with each vehicle.

The three pin connections were an earth at the top, a feed to the stop lamp at bottom left, and a feed to the tail lamp at bottom right.

Trafficators
When the 80-inch models were new, and for many years afterwards, it was common practice for drivers to use hand signals to indicate both an intention to stop and an intention to turn. Nevertheless, Lucas trafficators were an extra-cost option from at least October 1948, and possibly earlier.

These trafficators consisted of a black box with a sprung and illuminated semaphore arm in orange, and the type originally specified for the 80-inch was a Lucas SE62. There was a festoon type bulb inside each arm to provide the illumination. On the earliest vehicles, the trafficator box was bolted directly to the windscreen side frame near the top, but Rover soon added a mounting block to hold the box away from the side frame. The wiring that ran up the windscreen frame and was held to it by clips was normally protected by an armoured cable.

The control switch supplied for the trafficators was a black Lucas TS62 type and was mounted to a bracket on the inner edge of the windscreen frame bottom rail. This bracket was welded in place as standard from chassis number 86-0730 (some sources claim 86-0750), but for earlier vehicles the trafficator kit was supplied with a separate bracket that had to be bolted in place.

Tyre options
These are described in the Tyre section of the Chassis chapter.

Universal joint cover plates
Universal joint cover plates were available by July 1950, and were designed to prevent grass and vegetation getting caught in the universal joints as the propshaft revolved. They were typically fitted if the vehicle was used for stationary work in long grass.

The set of consisted of three cover plates. The two for the UJs on the front and rear differentials were the same, and were attached to the differential casing by a bolted strap plate. A different plate was provided for vehicles fitted with an oil cooler. The third plate was attached by drive screws under the transfer box and protected the UJs at either end.

Wheelbrace for split-rim wheels
A special wheelbrace was available to suit the nuts on the optional split-rim wheels.

Windscreen ventilator
The standard 80-inch windscreen had a fixed panel in the frame below the glass, but from June 1949 it was possible to order a hinged ventilator panel that fitted into the same space. It was possible to retro-fit the hinged panel, which simply bolted on in place of the fixed type.

The advantages of the hinged panel were that it could be opened to improve airflow through the vehicle, both to cool the occupants and to prevent dust and exhaust fumes from being drawn into the rear when driving with the rear curtain of the hood in the open position.

Windscreen wiper motor
A windscreen wiper motor for the passenger's side windscreen was an optional extra, as explained in the section on Electrical Equipment.

THE E CODES

Options and accessories that could be fitted on the assembly lines were identified by an E code that was specified on the vehicle's build sheet and alerted assembly line staff to the non-standard build. The E is believed to have stood for Extra, and a similar coding system was used for Rover cars.

The full list of codes associated with 80-inch models is not available, but the following are known to have been used:

E2	Rear PTO, drive section
E3	Pulley unit for rear PTO
E4	Centre PTO
E5	Engine governor
E6a	Pulley and fittings for E4
E6b	Pulley and fittings for E4 when E2 is also fitted
E7	Full-length removable metal top (hardtop)
E8	Five detachable rim wheels
E9	Five 700x16 Dunlop Tractor Tread tyres
E10	Chaff guard
E11	Rear winch (for use with E2) – by April 1950
E12	Thermometer and oil gauge
E14	Electric heater – Clayton type, by August 1949
E15a	Bonnet spare wheel carrier for 600x16 tyre
E15b	Bonnet spare wheel carrier for 700x16 tyre
E18	Windscreen ventilator – from June 1949
E23	Trafficators – by October 1948
E25	Cover plates for universal joints
E27	Brockhouse 15cwt trailer
E28	Heavy-duty army-type pintle hook
E31	Oil cooler (for use with E34)
E34	15 lb radiator pressure cap (for use with E31)

MILITARY MODIFICATIONS – 80-INCH

The 80-inch models supplied to the War Department from December 1948 were the first military Land Rovers in the world, and as a result set a pattern for others to follow. However, there was never any such thing as a standard military specification, because different military authorities had different requirements. Military vehicles of all kinds have always been modified in service, and therefore survivors will reflect those modifications and will not necessarily represent accurately the way the vehicles were when freshly delivered.

This chapter deliberately confines itself to the 80-inch Land Rovers delivered to the British armed forces and is intended to show the main elements of the ex-factory specification and to give some idea of how the vehicles were modified in

All the first Army deliveries and a few in the BC registration series had the serial number stencilled in white on the bonnet sides. This restored example displays the semaphore trafficators found on many Army 80-inch models. If the vehicle was used for front-line duties, the bumper would have been painted black; the galvanised parts would normally have been painted over, too.

MILITARY MODIFICATIONS – 80-INCH

Military vehicles were fitted with military contract plates. This one was for 04 BC 25, a 1950 model with chassis number R0610-1394, and both numbers are stamped into the plate.

service. There is more information on the British military 80-inch models in *British Military Land Rovers, the Leaf-Sprung models*, by James Taylor and Geoff Fletcher (Herridge & Sons, 2015).

The 80-inch models were delivered to all three armed services, through the intermediary of the Ministry of Supply. All of them had right-hand drive. The 1.6-litre 80-inch was known to the War Department as a Mk 1, and there were 2331 of them for the Army, 274 for the RAF and 16 for the Royal Navy. The 2.0-litre models were known as Mk 2 types and there were 2100 for the Army, 969 for the RAF, and 37 for the Royal Navy. Note that, in the absence of detailed records, the figures shown here for the RAF and Royal Navy are calculated minimum quantities.

Although the 1.6-litre Mk 1 and 2-litre Mk 2 models were essentially adapted civilian vehicles, their specification was by no means identical to that of a typical vehicle sold on the domestic civilian market.

Land Rovers reached the Army through the Ministry of Supply in the days of the 80-inch. This is the MoS plate on the inner front wing of a 1952 model, 2610-4724 (17 BH 65). The columns were stamped with dates of overhaul as confirmation that work had been done.

Identification

These 80-inch models were identified to the military authorities by a serial number that was displayed in place of the registration number used on civilian vehicles. Two types were used. The first type was used only on the batch of 20 evaluation vehicles supplied in December 1948, and was painted in white on the bonnet sides and tailgate. The serial numbers ran from M6279781 to M6279800.

For Army and RAF vehicles, the second type was a six-character number where the first pair and last pair were part of a sequential number series between 0001 and 9999, and the middle pair were identifying letters. A typical Army example (on the first of the summer 1949 deliveries) was 00 BC 01; identifying letters were BC or BD for the 1.6-litre models, and BD or BH for the 2-litre types. The RAF identifying letters were always AA. These numbers were normally displayed in white on black plates at the front and rear of the vehicle, although a few early 1.6-litre models in the BC series had their numbers painted on the bonnet sides in the earlier fashion.

The Royal Navy vehicles used a different numbering system, with the identifying letters RN preceded or followed by a four-digit number; 1003 RN would have been typical. These numbers were normally displayed on black plates at the front and rear. The Royal Navy later changed to a system similar to the Army and RAF type, always using RN as the middle letters, and it is likely that some 80-inch models were renumbered in this series. A typical example would have been 38 RN 17.

Army vehicles (and possibly also the RAF and Royal Navy deliveries) carried a rectangular brass plate on the left-hand side of the bulkhead in the engine compartment (right-hand side when standing looking at the engine). This showed the chassis number, the serial number, and the number of the contract under which the vehicle was supplied. A second and larger brass Ministry Of Supply plate was sometimes screwed to the inner wing, with spaces for a record of repairs, major maintenance and the workshop responsible.

Chassis, fittings, wheels and tyres

The chassis frame of all these vehicles had the standard civilian specification of the time, but was probably painted black from the start of deliveries. However, the Army had specifically requested deletion of the drawbar that was standard on civilian vehicles, and none of their vehicles had it. The front bumper was normally painted black in service, but some vehicles retained the galvanised finish, particularly RAF and Royal Navy

145

FACTORY-ORIGINAL LAND ROVER SERIES I, 80-INCH MODELS

The RAF saw no need to paint the galvanised fittings and did not do so. A bonnet-mounted spare wheel and semaphore indicators were standard, and this early example has the characteristic RAF roundel on the front wing, as well as various unit markings – and tyre pressure markings above the wheel arches. (Garth Teagle)

11 BC 57 was pictured in military use, complete with stencilled movement details on the windscreen. Note how all the galvanised body cappings have been painted over. There is just one windscreen wiper, and the driver's mirror is a military type with a rectangular body.

This 1951 model with the "lights-through" grille again displays a black bumper. In this case, the serial number is carried on the left-hand front wing, and there is also a separate rear-view mirror mounted on that wing. The spare wheel mounting on the bonnet has not been painted over, perhaps because it was normally concealed by the spare wheel itself.

vehicles, and some Army vehicles that would not be used for front-line duties.

Many 80-inch models supplied to the Army had a towing jaw assembly on the rear cross-member, although this appears not to have been universal; it may also be that the towing jaw was removed by individual units during service if it was not required. The towing jaw itself was drawn from the standard civilian options list.

All British military 80-inch Land Rovers initially had a three-pin civilian-pattern lighting socket with adaptor on the right-hand side of the rear cross-member. In later service, and particularly after 1956, some vehicles were re-equipped with a Warner socket so that they could tow the newer military-specification two-wheel trailers that were then entering service.

Most vehicles were delivered with standard disc wheels, although a few had the split-rim wheel option when in service and were presumably delivered in that condition. The British Army chose a non-standard 6.50 x 16 cross-country tyre as its standard fit, but it is possible that the Land Rovers delivered to the RAF and RN had standard 6.00 x 16 tyres and that these were also fitted to some of those delivered to the Army.

Engine and transmission

As delivered by Rover, all the British military 80-inch models had completely standard engines and transmissions.

The British Army did have 33 vehicles from the early 80-inch deliveries converted to use the 2.8-litre Rolls-Royce B40 engine, in order to get some experience of this engine (which was intended for the Austin Champ) in service. However, all these vehicles were originally supplied with the then-standard 1.6-litre engine, and Rover had nothing to do with the conversions, which were done under contract to the Army by

MILITARY MODIFICATIONS – 80-INCH

The poor fit of the bonnet panel gives a clue that this is one of the British Army vehicles converted for trials of the Rolls-Royce B40 engine, which was a tight squeeze in the engine bay. The cut-outs in the grille were a common Army modification to improve the performance of the headlights, which would have been located behind the grille when this Land Rover was new.

Hudson Motors Ltd of Chiswick in London.

The B40 engines were drawn from a batch of 50, of which 17 were for spares. The engines had serial numbers B40-518, B40-53x (exact number unknown), B40-556 to B40-605, and B40-609 to B40-610.

Bodywork

All the British military 80-inch models were delivered with a full-length canvas hood in the standard civilian colour of khaki. A few vehicles were fitted with a metal hardtop in service after this became available in February 1950, but it is not clear whether these hardtops were added after delivery to the War Department or were part of the ex-factory specification.

All the Land Rovers delivered to the Army, and probably those for the RAF and Royal Navy as well, were fitted with the optional windscreen ventilator panel. They also had the optional bonnet mounting for the spare wheel. Rover provided a special clamping plate kit so that the standard spare wheel carrier in the back body could be used as a jerrycan holder when the spare wheel was mounted on the bonnet.

With the exception of a 1948 evaluation batch of 20 vehicles, the 80-inch models for all three armed services were fitted with the optional guard rails fitted to the tail panel cappings. These appear to have been standard right across the board, and were retained even on the RAF vehicles that were equipped (by the RAF itself) as airfield crash rescue tenders and did not have the inward-facing rear seats (see below).

Army vehicles normally carried a yellow bridge plate (which indicated their weight classification to the bridgemaster who supervised a convoy crossing a bridge). This was fitted to the nose of the right-hand front wing and would be painted with an appropriate code number in black. Rover themselves actually supplied this metal plate for some of the military 80-inch models, and it had Rover part number 206818 (which was not listed in civilian parts catalogues).

From the start, the British Army wanted its Land Rovers delivered in Deep Bronze Green, which was the standard "home" colour for all its vehicles. It also wanted the chassis painted in black. The 20-strong evaluation batch in December 1948 met these criteria, and so did all the 1.6-litre 80-inch models that followed. It was in fact the Army's requirement for Deep Bronze Green that led to Rover making this colour standard in place of Light Green from summer 1949. Most of the Army's 2-litre 80-inch models were also delivered in Deep Bronze Green, but 850 of those ordered in 1951 were delivered with Light Stone paint, presumably for service in Middle

A tight squeeze indeed…. the 2.8-litre Rolls-Royce engine was nevertheless made to fit very well. Clear here is one of the rubber buffers fitted to the wings to allow the bonnet to stand up higher than normal in order to clear the larger radiator.

Eastern and Far Eastern theatres.

The RAF took many vehicles in its favoured blue-grey livery but also took vehicles in the standard Deep Bronze Green. The Royal Navy's standard vehicle colour was dark blue, but some of its 80-inch Land Rovers were delivered in bright yellow or orange for rôles where high visibility was important.

Electrical and lighting

Generally speaking, the electrical system on 80-inch Land Rovers delivered to the British armed services was to factory civilian standard, although heavy-duty items were fitted where they were available on civilian production. Like their civilian counterparts, the British military 80-inch models were delivered with a single Lucas CW1 wiper motor on the driver's side, although a second motor was sometimes fitted in service.

It is probable that all the 80-inch Land Rovers were delivered with standard civilian-pattern lights, although some vehicles certainly gained FV-pattern headlights during service. According to the User Handbook, the headlights were behind the grille up to chassis number 0611-2000, which would have been a 1.6-litre model registered in the BD sequence (the change to the new "lights-through" grille had occurred at chassis number 0611-1547 on production). Some of the early models had sections of the grille cut away in service, perhaps mainly to improve access for cleaning and changing bulbs, and a few were supposedly modified in service with the later grille and lights.

Many vehicles had an outside mirror mounted on the windscreen pillar, and on the evaluation batch of 20 vehicles this had a circular body on a cranked arm that was longer and provided a greater range of adjustment than the civilian type. Later vehicles had a rectangular type with a black body, again on a cranked arm. Some 80-inch models had wing mirrors, but these were probably fitted in service to meet the requirements of the parent unit.

Many vehicles – though perhaps not all – were delivered with the Lucas SE62 semaphore trafficators that were an extra-cost option on civilian vehicles. However, these were removed in

MILITARY MODIFICATIONS – 80-INCH

some theatres of operation for obvious reasons.

Some 80-inch models were fitted with a convoy light during service. This was mounted on a bracket behind the rear crossmember and shone onto the rear face of the differential, which was painted white. With the light on, a following driver could then see the vehicle ahead even when the main lights were off during blackout conditions. The switch for the convoy light was mounted to the dash or, in some cases, to the rear crossmember. The white face of the differential sometimes carried black-painted numbers, either to identify the vehicle's parent unit or to show the type of oil to be used in servicing.

A few vehicles were fitted in service with radio transmitting and receiving equipment, the initial trials probably dating from 1951. The electrical modifications associated with this were always made by the parent unit or by a REME unit on its behalf, and were not carried out by Rover.

Interior and fittings

The 1948 evaluation batch of 20 vehicles probably had only two seats in the cab instead of the standard complement of three, leaving the centre of the seatbox free for equipment stowage. These vehicles did not have the inward-facing bench seats in the rear or (as noted above) the guard rails that went with them.

When Land Rovers were ordered in quantity, only two seats were fitted in the cab. The Army deliveries all had the inward-facing rear seats, which appear to have been standard on the Royal Navy deliveries as well. They were accompanied as standard by the optional guard rails fitted to the tail panel cappings. As noted above, many of the RAF vehicles were fitted out as airfield crash rescue tenders and did not have the rear seats, even though they had the guard rails.

A standard fitting on the 80-inch models for all three services was a brass Pyrene fire extinguisher that was mounted on a bracket attached to the cab side of the bulkhead. The bracket was unmarked, but the extinguisher itself carried WD identification and a date, and was usually painted to match the vehicle's exterior.

Not every British Army 80-inch was painted green! The peculiar circumstances in which the Berlin Brigade operated required a large Military Police contingent to provide convoy escort duties within the city, and the escort vehicles were painted black. For parade use, white seat covers were added, and whitewall tyres were a common addition. The owner of this preserved example has carefully recreated the way the vehicle looked in service.

CKD MODELS

Not every 80-inch Land Rover left the Solihull factory as a fully assembled vehicle. Some export territories placed high import taxes on vehicles brought in from overseas, but encouraged in-territory assembly of vehicles because this provided work for the local labour force. So from mid-1949, Rover began to ship 80-inch models to such territories as kits of parts for local assembly. These vehicles were known as CKD types, the letters standing for Completely Knocked Down.

Some of these overseas assembly operations added a proportion of locally manufactured content to the material sent out from Solihull, although the proportions varied from one plant to another. Items such as tyres, glass, paint and batteries were typically (but not invariably) sourced locally. One result of this system is that some CKD vehicles have minor differences from those that were fully built up at Solihull.

The numbers of CKD chassis that left Solihull gradually increased during the years of 80-inch production. The figures for the 1950 and 1951 seasons are best estimates, but for 1952 and 1953 they may be considered reliable. There were probably 1213 during the 1950 season and 1024 for the 1951 season. For 1952 the figure was 3077; and for 1953 it was 9390.

Australia was a major CKD market in the days of the 80-inch Land Rovers. This is Car Zero, the first 80-inch to be fully restored by JLR Classic. It started life as a 1951-model CKD vehicle for Australia.

CKD MODELS

The first CKD Land Rovers were 1950 models, and shipping from Solihull began in August 1949. The earliest assembly operations were in Australia, Eire, and India. The records show that South Africa and Denmark followed in 1950, although there is some dispute about whether the Danish operation ever existed. More assembly operations followed in Belgium (1951) and Mexico (1952).

The 1950-model CKD 80-inch Land Rovers cannot be identified as CKD types from their chassis numbers alone, because these were drawn from the standard build sequences. However, dedicated CKD chassis sequences were created for the 1951, 1952 and 1953 models. Although vehicles would have been shipped in groups with a set of chassis numbers to cover them, it may be that each individual chassis was not stamped with its number until the assembly process had begun. As a result, at least one Australian-assembled vehicle was completed without its number stamped into the chassis. Similarly, the 80-inch models assembled by Annand & Thompson in Australia had the number stamped into the chassis rail just ahead of the engine mounting instead of in the usual place on the mounting. There may have been other variations.

The first CKD models were shipped in batches of anywhere between two and five vehicles, but by January 1950 Rover had standardised on batches of six. This was probably because this quantity made the most economical use of shipping space.

Retained on Car Zero pictured opposite is the plate applied by the supplying dealer in Australia. Annand & Thompson also built the vehicle up from CKD.

As time went on, local manufacture of some items increased. These pictures show an Australian-manufactured wheel, which bears the name of the maker and the standard Rover part number.

THE 80-INCH CKD OPERATIONS

Australia

Rover had divided the Australian territory into five regions, each of which was overseen by a Master Distributor. Four of these Master Distributors set up CKD assembly operations during 1949 and continued to build 80-inch models from CKD kits until they were replaced by the 86-inch models. The fifth Master Distributor was Faulls Motors of Perth, who were responsible for Western Australia, and they always took fully built export Land Rovers because they did not have the necessary assembly facilities.

The first CKD Land Rovers were shipped to Regent Motors of Melbourne in late August 1949, and records show the very first CKD Land Rover of all as having chassis number 0610-1396. Deliveries to Annand & Thompson of Brisbane began a week later, in early September. Then deliveries to Grenville Motors of Sydney and to Champion Motors in Adelaide began at the end of October.

These early Australian assembly operations seem to have been very straightforward, and not to have added a significant amount of local content to the kits shipped out from Solihull. However, Annand & Thompson stencilled the Land Rover name in yellow onto the front and rear of the Land Rovers they distributed, and Grenville Motors attached their own metal badge to the left front wing of each Land Rover.

Belgium
The details of the Belgian assembly operation, which was run by Minerva, are in the next chapter.

Denmark
The Rover despatch records suggest that some 1950 models were shipped to Denmark in CKD form, and make quite clear that all the 1951-model 1663-series chassis went to Skandinavsk Motors in Copenhagen. However, research has failed to unearth any evidence of a Land Rover CKD operation in that country. This therefore remains a mystery. A possible explanation is that

WHERE DID THEY GO?

1950 season
- 0610- and 0611-series — Australia (RHD)
- Denmark (LHD)
- Eire (RHD)
- India (RHD)

1951 season
- 1663-series (LHD) — Denmark
- 1666-series (RHD) — South Africa

1952 season
- 2663-series (LHD) — Belgium (Minerva), Mexico
- 2666-series (RHD) — Australia, Eire, India

1953 season
- 3663-series (LHD) — Belgium (Minerva), Mexico
- 3666-series (RHD) — Australia, Eire, India, South Africa

Australian dealer Annand & Thompson, which ran the CKD operation in Brisbane, painted a large identifier on the tailboard to help publicise the Land Rover. Here it is on a 1951 Welder.

Grenville Motors of Sydney applied this badge to the front wing of about 300 Land Rovers in 1948-1950. The background to the letters was originally red.

the 1663-series was not used for CKD vehicles as originally planned, but was instead devoted to Danish exports. That is nevertheless no more than a guess.

Eire

Northern Ireland was treated as a part of the UK and received fully built vehicles direct from Solihull, but the Republic of Ireland (Eire) was treated as an export market.

The first 80-inch models left Solihull for Eire on 18 November 1949, and were assembled by Lincoln & Nolan, of Lower Baggot Street in Dublin. This company had been assembling Rover cars from CKD since 1948, and Land Rover assembly was carried out alongside that of other British cars, including the Morris Minor. This was always a small assembly operation, and the quantities of Land Rovers were sometimes tiny.

India

Rover's representatives in India were Dewar's Garage and Engineering Works of Calcutta, who set up a Land Rover assembly operation during 1949. The first 80-inch models were shipped to India from Solihull on 28 November 1949. There was a pause in deliveries during the 1951 season, but CKD shipments to India resumed with the 1952-season 2-litre models. Very little detail is available about the 80-inch models assembled in India.

Mexico

CKD assembly began in Mexico in the second quarter of 1952. The first kits were shipped to Autoproductos at the beginning of April, and were followed by some for Reforma at the beginning of May. For the 1953 models, there were three destination addresses: Societa Distribution Auto (from mid-August 1952), Auto Panhard (from early September), and Automoviles Ingleses (from mid-March 1953). Whether this reflected real changes in the destination or simply changes of name by the assemblers is not clear. There is currently no further information available about the 80-inch models assembled in Mexico.

South Africa

Deliveries to South Africa began at the end of August 1950, for assembly by Car Assembly of East London. The despatch records show a change of name for the assembly operation in January 1951, to Car Distribution and Assembly, and then during February three further branches of the same company began to receive CKD kits, at Durban, Windhoek and Johannesburg.

GRIP, MINERVA & TEMPO

Rescued, but not yet restored: this is a Grip 80-inch, with a large sun visor that was not a standard feature.

There were three very special derivatives of the 80-inch Land Rover that were assembled overseas, and although full details of each one remain tantalisingly out of reach nearly 70 years after they were first built, it is important to acknowledge their existence here.

The three special derivatives were produced by Grip in Sweden, by Minerva in Belgium, and by Tempo in Germany. Each one of the three operated a different system. Minerva was supplied with CKD vehicles, Tempo took part-completed vehicles, but the Grip Land Rovers were conversions of fully-built vehicles.

GRIP

From an early date, 80-inch Land Rovers were exported to Sweden, where they were handled by ABA Wiklund in Stockholm. It soon became clear that the poor weather protection of the standard model was a deterrent to sales in a country where the winters were long and bitterly cold, and Wiklund decided to make some local improvements to help sales.

The company engaged the help of a small specialist company in Stockholm called Gripkarosserier AB (more familiarly, Grip). Grip was a specialist in cab heating and demisting equipment,

FACTORY-ORIGINAL LAND ROVER SERIES I, 80-INCH MODELS

and its products were used on many Swedish-built trucks. It appears that the company first developed a high-output cab heater for the Land Rover, but before long supplemented this with a fully enclosed and insulated coachbuilt cab. This cab was available by 1952 and was coachbuilt, with steel panels over a wooden frame.

The Grip cab was considerably larger than the Truck Cab that Land Rover offered as an option. Like the Tickford Station Wagon, it had structural timbers bolted to each outer side of the bulkhead, with the result that the body overhung the sides of the chassis. It also extended backwards into the area normally occupied by the load-bed. This of course compromised the carrying capacity, and although some customers were content with the shorter load bed, others were not. For them, Grip modified the tub, in effect mounting it backwards to give a longer rear overhang. Later, the wheelbase was also extended for some variants.

There are no reliable production figures for these distinctive conversions, but from the recollections of a former Grip employee it is likely that around 40 examples a year were made.

The principal characteristic of the Grip conversions was the large and weather-proof cab. This early example was a service vehicle for the city of Stockholm, and had an extended body tub as well.

In this case, the back body has the standard length, but is still overlapped at the front by the special cab.

An important element in the Grip cab was this heater unit, which was considerably more effective than the one offered as an option by Rover.

The new Grip cab was constructed on a wooden frame.

The Belgian armed forces were the primary user of the Minerva-built 80-inch models. The most obvious identifying feature on this 1952 example is the angled front to the wings. The freewheeling front hubs would not have been fitted when the vehicle was new.

MINERVA

The Belgian Minerva company had been a respected maker of luxury cars before the 1939-1945 war, but its traditional market had collapsed after 1945. It returned to business with a licence-building arrangement for the British Standard Vanguard saloon, and then in 1951 negotiated a deal to provide Land Rovers to the Belgian military and Gendarmerie.

The arrangement was that the Rover Company would provide complete chassis, but without body panels, and Minerva would then build the bodies to meet the special requirements of the customers. Assembly would be at the Minerva factory in Mortsel, near Antwerp. Rover despatch records show that 1895 part-completed 80-inch models in the 2663 chassis series were supplied to Minerva during the 1952 season, and a further 6910 in the 3663 series followed in 1953.

Not all of these 8805 Land Rovers went to the Belgian authorities. As far as it is possible to tell, 8440 did so, and Minerva then renegotiated the contract with the Rover Company, expanding its activities by building a further 365 80-inch Land Rovers for sale on the civilian market.

Minerva built them all up with steel bodies that had a unique specification, and badged them as Land Rover Minerva types. They had sloping front wings, a unique grille and a fixed rear panel instead of a drop-down tailgate. Minerva also changed their electrical systems to use twin 6-volt batteries instead of a single 12-volt type, and to use a negative earth instead of the positive earth standard on UK-built models. (Some of the first ones may nevertheless have retained the original single-battery system.)

A further contract for partial Belgian manufacture of 86-inch models followed in 1954.

FACTORY-ORIGINAL LAND ROVER SERIES I, 80-INCH MODELS

Minerva models were also used by the Belgian Rijkswacht or Gendarmerie. All the Minerva 80s had the same angled door trailing edge as the British-built originals, as well as an inside door release. (Paul Theys)

The Minerva exhaust discharged ahead of the left-hand rear wheel, and the rear panel was fixed. It carried a jerrycan and the spare wheel. (Paul Theys)

The front panel and grille of the Minerva were unique, and the rust on this one underlines the fact that they were made of steel.

Electrical equipment was sourced in Belgium, and differed from the Lucas items used on British-built 80-inch models.

The Minerva models also had a special grille badge.

There was a considerable time lag before some Minervas were assembled. The plate makes clear that this 1953-model 3663-series vehicle was not actually built up until 1954.

The Tempo 80-inch built in Germany for the BGS again had a steel body. Clear in this picture are the tall doors, the locker mounted on the bonnet, and the stowage boxes let into the front wings.

TEMPO

After the Second World War, Germany was divided into a western sector controlled by the Allies and an eastern sector controlled by the Soviet Union. Although West Germany was forbidden under the terms of its 1945 surrender to raise a standing army of its own, it soon became clear that it needed to protect its border with the Soviet-controlled German Democratic Republic. The West German authorities therefore established a special force called the BGS (Bundesgrenzschutz, or Federal Border Police).

During 1952, the BGS invited tenders for 250 4x4 patrol vehicles to use along the Inner German Border, and the winning contender was the Land Rover. However, the BGS called for a unique specification that would enable the vehicles to carry six troops plus radio equipment and sundry other items. Building these on the assembly lines at Solihull would have been hugely disruptive, and so the Rover Company made an arrangement similar to the one with Minerva in Belgium. Rover would supply part-built Land Rovers (essentially rolling chassis with bulkheads, bonnets and front panels) and these would be specially adapted by Vidal und Sohn of Hamburg, who were

Even though the doors had a very different design from the standard type, they still retained the characteristic sloping rear edge of the 80-inch.

The Tempo seats had tubular frames and were totally different from the standard type. As is clear here, the Tempo had no seatbox, either.

known for their light commercial vehicles under the Tempo brand name.

The part-built chassis were numbered in the 3613 series, and the first ones left Solihull for Hamburg in January 1953. By April (some sources say February) the first completed Tempo Land Rovers came off the assembly line in Hamburg. Tempo made some modifications to the chassis before fitting their special bodies. The electrical systems were changed to negative earth to suit the use of two-way radios, and used Bosch components, while the under-seat fuel tank was removed and replaced by twin rear-mounted tanks.

Manufacture of the special bodies for the Tempo vehicles was sub-contracted to Herbert Vidal und Sohn, a coachwork company run by the brother of Tempo's owner, Oscar Vidal. These bodies had a troop-carrier configuration, and were made from steel. They were distinguished by a high waistline, with the doors and back body reaching the level of the bottom of the windscreen frame. There was a fixed rear panel, with a filler for the rear-mounted fuel tanks, a carrier for the spare wheel and a bracket for carrying a jerrycan, and the standard D-shaped tail lamps were mounted lower down than on standard bodies.

Both front wings were modified to incorporate lidded lockers in the front ends, and brackets were added to the wing tops to carry a shovel and an axe. On top of the bonnet, a large steel locker provided stowage for the removable door tops, and a front-mounted capstan winch was standard. Door handles were different from the Solihull type and so was the tilt, which had a single flexible window in each side and in the rear curtain, and was attached to a folding frame rather than

The fuel tank was relocated at the rear, with an external filler, and the spare wheel was also mounted on the rear panel.

The steel panels were strong enough to take the hinges, straps and turnbuckles of the stowage boxes.

the fixed hoodsticks of the standard 80-inch.

The Tempo 80-inch models had two tubular-framed front seats mounted directly to the floor (there was no seatbox), and the space between them was reserved for radio equipment. The seats hinged forwards and their backrests folded down to give access to the rear compartment, while a locker under the one on the right made good use of the space freed up by moving the fuel tank. Many Tempos were probably fitted with a separate heater to make winter patrol work more bearable. The back body, meanwhile, contained inward-facing bench seats for four BGS troops, and there was a slatted wooden floor section retained in a central recess. A special gun-rack was mounted to the inside of the rear panel.

Some BGS Tempos were fitted with a tall telescopic radio mast between the fuel filler neck and the spare wheel, but it is not clear whether this was fitted when they were new or was an upgrade made in the early 1960s. As Police vehicles, they carried a blue beacon and two sirens which were located underneath the front sidelights and were controlled from an extra switch panel mounted above the main instrument panel.

Production numbers of these vehicles remain unclear. The Land Rover Despatch Records show that 189 1953 models were shipped to Tempo, but some German sources claim that no more than 100 80-inch Tempos entered BGFS service (and others claim a figure of 178). There is no obvious explanation of the discrepancy. Once 80-inch production had ended, Tempo went on to build a quantity of similar vehicles for the BGS on 86-inch chassis.

All the plates on the dashboard were printed in German, including the instruction plate for the transfer box, seen here in the middle.